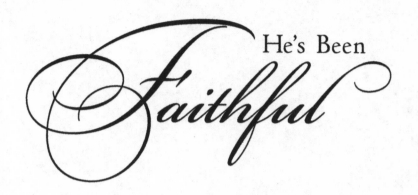

He's Been
Faithful

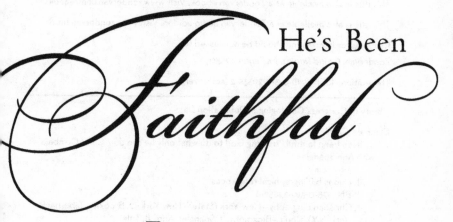

He's Been

Faithful

Trusting God
to Do What Only He Can Do

CAROL CYMBALA

Director of the Grammy Award-Winning Brooklyn Tabernacle Choir

with Ann Spangler

ZONDERVAN®

ZONDERVAN.com/
AUTHORTRACKER
follow your favorite authors

ZONDERVAN

He's Been Faithful
Copyright © 2001 by Carol Cymbala

This title is also available as a Zondervan ebook. Visit www.zondervan.com/ebooks.

This title is also available in a Zondervan audio edition. Visit www.zondervan.fm.

Requests for information should be addressed to:
Zondervan, *Grand Rapids, Michigan* 49530

This edition: ISBN 978-0-310-29339-2 (softcover)

Library of Congress Cataloging-in-Publication Data

Cymbala, Carol.
    He's been faithful : trusting God to do what only he can do / Carol Cymbala
with Ann Spangler.
        p.   cm.
    Includes bibliographical references.
    ISBN 978-0-310-23652-8
    1. Christian biography—New York (State)—New York. 2. Brooklyn Tabernacle
(New York, N.Y.). Choir—Biography. I. Spangler, Ann. II. Title.
BR1700.3 .C95 2001
277.47'1'083—dc21   2001026744

The author and publisher would like to thank the music companies who granted per-
mission to quote the following songs:
  "God Is Working," "Nothing Is Impossible," "Make Us One," and "He's Been Faithful" © Carol Joy
  Music. Used with permission.
  "More Than Enough" © by Robert Gay and Prophetic Praise Ministries. Used with permission.
  "Favorite Song of All" by Dan Dean © Dawn Treader Music. Used with permission.

Published in association with the literary agency of Ann Spangler and Company, 1420
Pontiac Road SE, Grand Rapids, MI 49506

Interior design: Melissa Elenbaas

Printed in the United States of America

HB 08.23.2017

To my three children, Chrissy, Susan, and James,

who are deeply loved and cherished as special gifts from God.

They have seen as children and now experience as adults

that he's been faithful.

To my husband, Jim, who has been a constant

source of love and encouragement in my life.

CONTENTS

CONTENTS

ACKNOWLEDGMENTS

Most books come into the world, not as orphans, but as members of a publishing family. We are particularly grateful for ours. Special thanks go to Scott Bolinder for his initial support of the project and to Cindy Hays whose encouragement, prayers, and insight have been invaluable, especially during those times when our confidence wavered. We also want to thank Robert Hudson for his skillful and sensitive editing of the manuscript. But even the best-edited manuscript would have a hard time making its way into the world of books without the help of careful marketing. In that regard, we are particularly grateful to John Topliff and his creative team for their efforts in introducing the book to as many people as possible.

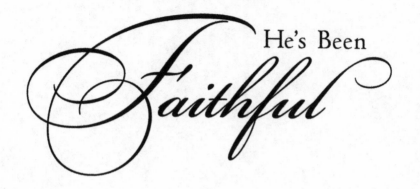

He's Been

Faithful

NOTHING IS IMPOSSIBLE

As I swerve in and out of traffic on Brooklyn's busy streets, it's hard to ignore the bumper stickers pasted onto every car but mine. A few are thought-provoking, others are funny, and some are too nasty to mention. But that's to be expected in a city like New York, which is not exactly famous for its modesty. If I ever put a bumper sticker on my car, it will probably read: "She doesn't know what she's doing, she just keeps doing it." That's the joke about me that circulates in the Brooklyn Tabernacle, the church my husband, Jim, and I have loved and labored over for the past twenty-nine years.

But despite—or maybe because of—my many inadequacies, I've seen God do some amazing things. Sunday after Sunday, as I direct the 275-member Brooklyn Tabernacle Choir, my eyes rest on a sea of faces—brown, black, and white—each concealing a remarkable story, each holding an incredible tale. Later, as I sit at the piano, I see men and women throughout the church, faces shining, voices raised, and I am once again grateful to be here. It's where I'm happiest. It's where I belong.

I've lived all my life in church. My father, Clair Hutchins, was an opera-singer-turned-pastor. I can remember as a four-year-old, sitting on his knee, listening to a visiting preacher.

I don't remember what he said, but I'll never forget what I experienced. God's presence was so real that I felt overwhelmed. It left me with a hunger that has shaped my life.

Yes, I love the church, but not because it has formed a snug cocoon around me, insulating me from the world. Just the opposite is true. It's where I've encountered my fears. It's where my faith has grown larger; pushing me over edges I didn't want to get near. It's forced me to try things that scared me to death—speaking in public, conducting the choir in front of thousands of people, giving an acceptance speech at the Grammy's, and writing this book. Maybe things like that come easily for others, but they're hard assignments for a person like me who has always preferred to stay in the background.

> *Yes, I love the church, but not because it has formed a snug cocoon around me, insulating me from the world. Just the opposite is true.*

At times, life in church has been anything but safe. Like the Sunday a man with a gun in his hand walked down the aisle toward my husband. Like the time a woman assaulted me outside of church. Like the Friday night nobody could leave the building after choir practice because of a gang fight going on right across the street.

Every day I rub shoulders with people who don't have a clue about my midwestern roots or my occasional longing to return to a more simple life in the middle of nowhere. How could they? They come from the busy streets of New York, from Trinidad, Jamaica, and Puerto Rico. A number of them have moved to America, hoping for a better life. Some have come from unimaginable poverty, while others are business people, doctors, and lawyers—all mixed up together in the wonderful family that forms our church.

And I'm tossed into the mix as well. An introvert among extroverts. A white woman in an ethnically diverse church. Never quite confident I can do what God wants me to. Certain, in fact, that I can't unless God does something. But the beautiful thing is that he does do something. Time and again. Over and over. He comes through. And that's what I want to tell you about—how God's been faithful, year after year, in every imaginable way. I hope my story and the stories of the people I love will stir you and point you to the only person worth looking at, the only one worth getting excited about. In doing so, I hope to share a few of the lessons I've learned along the way. I want to urge you to consider your own limitations not as obstacles but as opportunities for God to show his limitless power and unlimited love.

God's favor on the church and the choir has been incredible. He's been so good to us. How likely is it that someone who barely made it through high school and who can't even read a note of music would ever stand on the stage of Radio City Music Hall or Carnegie Hall? How likely is it that the choir would win four Grammy awards and record twenty albums? I'm not telling you this to impress you but to show you how God can create something beautiful out of our weakness.

This isn't a story about fame or the thrill of performance. The Brooklyn Tabernacle Choir doesn't perform. We haven't provided backup to musical superstars or sung at national political conventions, even though we've been asked to more than once. Our call, our greatest joy, is to worship God, and to lead other Christians to experience him in worship. We also want to sing the message of the gospel to those who don't know Christ. So week after week, we open our hearts to him, eagerly waiting, painfully aware that if God doesn't come to meet us, we will never accomplish our purpose.

We are not naïve about the dangers that come with apparent success, because we know that self-aggrandizement displeases God. And God won't bless us if we're out to please ourselves. I tell the choir, "God has allowed us to win four Grammys. But there are better choirs out there. The only reason he's blessed us is so he can use us to reach more people. So just remember who you are, and I'll remember who I am. Apart from God we're nothing."

So this is my story and the story of others who've touched my life. But it's really the story of what God can do despite— no, because of—our weakness. It's the story of how he loves us, of how he acts in surprising and marvelous ways to do what only he can do.

It's not always a glorious story either. Sometimes things get messy. Believe me, I have known some dark days. I promise to be as honest with you as a shy person can. There have been times I've wanted to run away from this city, taking my children with me to a saner, safer place. There have been spiritual attacks on my husband and myself. Times of doubt and illness for me. But through it all, God has given me the strength to stay and to stretch, to pray and to believe.

LIVE AT RADIO CITY

Living in New York isn't always hard work. It has its advantages, like being able to attend a rich variety of cultural events. There's Carnegie Hall, the Metropolitan Opera, Broadway's theater district, Madison Square Garden, and, of course, Radio City Music Hall, whose famous stage is designed to resemble a setting sun sinking into an ocean of red velvet seats. Normally a visit there is something to celebrate. But as I discovered, it's one thing to sit in the audience and another to anticipate directing the choir before a packed-out audience.

As I sat in my dressing room one evening in April 1987, just minutes before going onstage, I felt my heart sink into an ocean of worry.

The Brooklyn Tabernacle Choir had spent weeks rehearsing for its debut on the world's largest, most famous stage. Now, choir members stood in the basement of Radio City Music Hall, waiting to make the twenty-seven-foot ascent to the auditorium. The stage that would carry us up is supported by a hydraulic system once considered top secret because it influenced the design of aircraft carriers used during World War II. A full city-block wide, it would make for a memorable entrance.

Though God had given us a remarkable opportunity that evening, I wasn't smiling. At that moment, I would rather have climbed Mount Everest than set foot on stage. I felt blank, bone weary, and brain dead. The very first song, the one that would set the tone for the rest of the night, was tricky and hard to count through using the "click track" that synchronized the recorded orchestration with our live band. Every time we rehearsed, I had gotten the count wrong, bringing the drummer and choir in at just the wrong moment. If I missed it again tonight, I would make a fool of myself and the choir I loved in front of thousands of people.

I slumped further into my chair, realizing it was only fifteen minutes to curtain. "God, how am I going to do this?" It wasn't even a prayer, because I hadn't the energy or faith to pray.

Then, as I bent over to put on my shoes, the atmosphere of the room suddenly cleared, and I felt something come over me, rushing through me like a wave of light, clearing away the fog. Totally charged, I felt full of faith, able to do what I had to regardless of how great the pressure. I joined the rest of the choir already assembled on the giant elevator. As the stage began to rise, I felt ready for anything.

THE BIG CITY

No one is more surprised than I about the way God has worked in my life, especially when I think back to the first moment I laid eyes on New York. It was 1954, right in the middle of Eisenhower's first term in office. I was only six years old, a child stepping into a new world, unaware of anything beyond what was happening to myself and my family as we drove into the city one steamy August night. Even with the windows rolled down, it was so hot that my legs felt pasted to the vinyl seat of our blue 1954 Mercury. Whenever I tried to shift clear of the other sticky kids in the backseat, the skin on the back of my legs felt like tape peeling off a package. It must have been even more unpleasant for my pregnant mother, sitting in front next to my father.

"Who picked this place?" "We're moving here?" "There's no grass!" My older brother and sister and I chimed in as the city swung into view. We had come from midwestern roots, and New York at night was a shock for kids used to open spaces and large backyards. One of our first meals came as a shock as well. We'd never heard of pizza. Why would anybody combine cheese and tomato sauce with a whole bunch of weird stuff on a large flat crust that had been thrown up in the air and twirled around? What happened to pot roast and potatoes, fried chicken, green beans, and white bread with butter? This new food was strange and spicy, a surprising mix of ingredients just like the city itself.

My dad had accepted an invitation to become pastor of Maranatha Temple, a Scandinavian congregation in Brooklyn. Before that he had served as pastor of a church in Chicago.

A month after we arrived, I sat in Dad's office, a six-year-old girl with blond hair, perched on a table, waiting patiently while my mother pulled up my anklets and fastened the buckles on my Sunday-best shoes. All of a sudden, a young boy stuck his head around the corner and stared straight at me. That was my first look at little Jimmy Cymbala, a round-faced boy whose family joined the church shortly after we arrived. Jim was eleven and he and my brother, Richard, quickly became best friends. He spent most of his time at our house, treating me as a pesky little sister, nothing more.

Of the six children in my family, I think everyone would agree I was the least likely to grow up and do anything memorable. I was just so shy and insecure. I couldn't even bring myself to raise my hand in school.

If I could discard just one memory from those early days, I would toss out the day I took my first test. As the other first graders hunched over their papers, I sat quietly, doing nothing, not sure what I could do without a pencil to write with. Ten minutes passed before I worked up the courage to ask for one. When I did, the teacher let me have it, shouting and slamming a book onto her desk so hard I thought it would collapse. But it didn't. I fell apart instead. For a shy girl, unable to put words to her thoughts or feelings, this wasn't a great way to kick things off. School didn't click for me then or ever.

But being in church was totally different. I loved it. It brought so much excitement and happiness to my six-year-old life. And since anybody of any age could join the choir in those days, I did, pretending I could read and hoping I was fooling everybody as I held the big hymn book up to my face. Our little choir wasn't much, but at least it was backed up by a small string band and a piano.

Along with my family, I'd spend Wednesday and Friday nights and all day Sunday in church, much of the time kneeling at the altar after each service. Sometimes people would be there for long periods of time waiting on God. No one was thinking about the time because when you're in the presence of God there is no time. You never felt rushed. You never felt bored. You felt happy and at peace.

But as good as it was, my life in church was always overshadowed by the dread of school lying in wait for me on Monday morning.

Sometimes people would be there for long periods of time waiting on God. No one was thinking about the time because when you're in the presence of God there is no time. You never felt rushed. You never felt bored. You felt happy and at peace.

School was never a safe place for me, a place to be myself, to learn from my mistakes, and develop my talents. As far as I knew, I didn't have any talents anyway, at least not the school kind. I felt fearful, unable to measure up. I was a daydreamer, a child who loved creative things and working with her hands but who hated to study. That frightened first grader, in fact, typified my experience of life for a long time to come.

Given my deep level of insecurity, you may wonder what has kept me from painting my life into the smallest of corners, making my world a safe but narrow place? If you know anything about my husband, Jim, whose first book, *Fresh Wind, Fresh Fire,* tells the story of some of the ways God has worked in our lives, you'll realize how difficult it would have been for him to be married to someone who dug in her heels, refusing to take the risks God was asking. Still, it hasn't been my marriage that has pushed me out of my comfort zone. And it hasn't been my life circumstances. Instead, it's been my sense of God's incredible love. I simply wanted to love him back the best way I could, and I've always known that loving him meant saying yes, no matter how awkward or afraid I felt. I remember as a seventeen-year-old girl, praying, "God, whatever you want with my life, whatever you want me to do, I want to say yes to you." That's all it took.

It's true that I come from a musical family. My father's mother was a talented pianist and my dad recorded several albums. Still, my natural abilities have never been strong enough to carry me past my sense of inadequacy and my fear of the limelight.

In the early years, God asked small things of me, though they felt big enough at the time. As a teenager I played the piano and organ in my father's church. Later, when I was twenty-two, Jim and I were pastoring a small church in Newark, New Jersey, where I formed my very first choir. I had invited six middle-aged women to come to my home so I could teach them one simple song we could sing together in church. How hard could that be? But I felt so young and out of place, even though my husband was the pastor. Who was I to tell these women anything? I didn't eat the whole day, and was so nervous I got sick that afternoon before they came and was sick again after the women left. But I survived.

MORE CHALLENGES

By 1979, Jim and I were at the Brooklyn Tabernacle. By then I had about seventy choir members, and we decided to make our first recording. One thing led to another and I found myself at a studio in Manhattan where Frank Sinatra had recorded "New York, New York." My producer had wonderful credentials, having worked with Natalie Cole on a previous album. Since I had never been musically trained and didn't read music, my insecurities rose up again like the world's biggest mountain. But I played the piano and the producer brought in other professional musicians to provide the rhythm section. We started at 7:00 P.M. and finished at 2:20

A.M. The whole thing was done in less than eight hours—the choir, the solos, the rhythm track, everything but the orchestration. That was unheard of, but we did it anyway.

Then we went to Chicago to record the orchestra. I had one song that still needed a soloist so I asked a gospel singer I knew to sing it. The soloist sang in a way that showcased talent but displayed very little heart. To me the song was sacred, so I poked my head into the studio and asked if it could be sung a little straighter. Instead of smiling and nodding, the soloist turned and said, "Don't give me that garbage" and went on singing just as before. I didn't know how to respond. I was so crushed. This person had been trained and I hadn't. I only had my ear and heart to rely on. I let it pass.

> *Since I had never been musically trained and didn't read music, my insecurities rose up again like the world's biggest mountain.*

Later Word Music heard our first recording, liked it, and wanted the choir to sign a contract with them. That was 1981. Though Word helped us a great deal, those early years were painful. The Nashville musicians we worked with came from a totally white world and didn't have a clue about the kind of music we sang. They looked at me and saw a white woman, never imagining the real world I lived in.

I would write songs with a certain feel and rhythm only to have them changed when they were recorded. After completing an album, I would feel depressed. It didn't sound anything like the way we did the music in church. But I kept thinking, *What do I know? I can't say anything, because I'm not trained. They must know because this is what they do for a living.* Again my insecurity surfaced, hindering me from expressing what I felt in my heart.

Sometimes when I look back on my life, I have to laugh. How could six women in a little church in Newark make me freeze up? How could I have been so timid about those first few recordings? Anyone who knows me will tell you that today I haven't the slightest problem asserting myself when I feel the music is heading in the wrong direction. Such memories seem comic in light of the other things God has asked me to do since, like conducting the choir at Madison Square Garden or teaching thousands of choir directors across the country.

FEELING STRETCHED

Because of how God has worked in my life, I realize how crucial it is to yield to him. So many times our relationship with him grows stale because we are determined to hold onto our lives. We can become stubborn and egocentric. Or we become afraid the minute we feel stretched, upset, or awkward, so we shrink back. We think something must be wrong if we're feeling like that. The last thing any of us wants is to look foolish. We prefer to play it safe. We want to trust and obey Christ—but only so far.

But our desire to stay in control forces us to pay the highest price imaginable—letting our relationship with God gradually grow cold. Before long, we become mechanical and lose all sense of passion in serving the Lord. We can go through the motions, but our lives become hollow and our faith degenerates into mere surface religion.

Believe me, I don't enjoy telling you about the range of insecurities I suffer. This is not another human-interest story of how someone overcame great obstacles in order to live out the American Dream. If I've done anything worthwhile, it's only been by the grace of God. Because he shows himself strong when I am at my weakest. He uses my difficulties to shape me. It's a kind of sifting process that is anything but comfortable. Charles Spurgeon, the great pastor and preacher who lived in the 1800s and who battled serious depression, said that the secret of many men and women who have blessed others could be found in their response to the tremendous challenges *they themselves* had to battle. God blessed them and used them, not in spite of their difficulties but because of them.

> *But our desire to stay in control forces us to pay the highest price imaginable— letting our relationship with God gradually grow cold. Before long, we become mechanical and lose all sense of passion in serving the Lord.*

I can't help but think of how God used people in the Bible—Joseph was hated by his brothers and sold into slavery. Yet he became a leader in Egypt. Elizabeth had grown old in age and couldn't have children. Yet she became the mother of John the Baptist. Peter was a simple fisherman who preached to thousands on the day of Pentecost. Were any of these people self-made men and women? I don't think so. Their stories highlight not their own strength but the power and love of God in the midst of their limitations.

A. B. Simpson, in his book *The Holy Spirit,* reflects on the story of Moses in a way that really hits home for me. Even though Moses encountered God in the desert in a very dramatic way, he shrank back from doing what God asked because he felt inadequate, saying: "O Lord, I have never been eloquent, neither in the past nor since you have spoken to your servant. I am slow of speech and tongue." Boy, did that ever sound familiar! But God replied: "Who gave man his mouth? Who makes him deaf or mute? Who gives him sight or makes him blind? Is it not I, the Lord?" Still Moses kept it up: "O Lord, please send someone else to do it" (Exodus

4:10–14). Finally, God told Moses that his brother Aaron could become his spokesman.

What A. B. Simpson points out is that Moses' faith was too small—it wasn't large enough to match the promise God had made to him. So he shared his commission with his brother, and his brother actually made things a whole lot more difficult for him. It would have been so much easier if Moses had simply taken God at his word.

If you really want God to use you, then you have to be willing to follow him into uncomfortable places and to do things you simply can't do on a natural level. If all this sounds strange, you have to remember that God's ways are not ours. The life that Jesus offers is a supernatural life and it turns everything upside down making no sense at all to the natural mind. In his infinite wisdom, God does things in ways that wouldn't occur to us even if we had a million years to ponder them. He chooses the foolish to better display his wisdom. He chooses the weak to display his strength (1 Corinthians 1:26–29).

The story of my life involves doing the very things I dread. Not that I ever hated the thought of using my musical gifts or leading a choir. I had dreamt about leading a large choir since I was a child. But I never wanted the publicity, the attention that comes with it. I never wanted to get up on a stage and speak. But I've done it anyway and learned at least one thing as a result: though doing God's will hasn't always been easy, it has always been good. Always better than I imagined, taking me beyond my small plans to God's big

If you really want God to use you, then you have to be willing to follow him into uncomfortable places and to do things you simply can't do on a natural level.

plans. Because of his promise and proven faithfulness, I know that nothing is impossible for God.

HERE WE GO

When I walked onto the elevator that night at Radio City Music Hall, I was trembling. But it wasn't from nerves. "Lord, here we go," I said, as the elevator began to rise. The orchestra struck the first note and I started the count down. Would I get it right even though I'd missed it every other time? Dressed in white gowns and black tuxedos, we made our entrance in a swirl of smoke against the glittering backdrop of Manhattan at night. The rhythm section and the choir came in at precisely the right moment, and the audience rose in spontaneous applause. I felt as though I'd just been swept up to the top of the world's highest mountain. What a sight!

Later, I heard the stories of those who had been touched by the gospel, by the music and worship that filled Radio City Music Hall. People had come because they were attracted by the music but many left with a newfound faith in Jesus Christ. I knew that God, not Carol Cymbala, was the one who had orchestrated the events of that evening. He had used me despite my reluctance. And he had used each member of the choir, whose voices blended into a marvelous song of praise, to call broken men and women to himself.

A bachelor by the name of Bob Adamo was one of the people in the audience that night. A sales manager at IBM who lived in the posh district of Brooklyn Heights, he'd been invited by someone who worked in his office.

"Everybody thought I had it made. I had money, a beautiful place to live, a job I loved. People generally liked me, though for some reason, I never found the right girl to settle down with. In fact my life revolved around my job. There was nothing else to fill up my time. Though it looked like I was living the American Dream, I began to feel pretty dissatisfied, even depressed. I actually thought about suicide a lot but didn't have the nerve to kill myself. So work became my coping mechanism. I just let it swallow me up so I didn't have to face myself, didn't have to deal with the depression I felt. If anybody noticed anything wrong, they just figured I was lonely and needed a girlfriend. But it wasn't that simple.

"After a while I developed a friendship with someone at work who talked to me about God. She had invited me to visit the Brooklyn Tabernacle more than once, but I always had an excuse. Finally she invited me to a concert at Radio City Music Hall. That was okay. After all, it was Radio City, not a church.

"The one thing she failed to mention was that this wasn't your ordinary concert but one where somebody would stand up and preach. I wasn't prepared for that. I don't even remember what Pastor Cymbala said that night, but after listening to the choir and hearing his words, I knew I had a choice to make. So I stood up the minute he asked people who wanted to accept Christ to stand for prayer.

"After that I started to attend the Brooklyn Tabernacle and even joined the choir, and that's amazing because I don't have that good a voice and it's hard to get into the choir. I keep hoping Carol won't discover her mistake, because I can't help thinking she must have mixed me up with someone else when I auditioned. But I guess I've just blown my cover, haven't I?

"Anyway, after a while my depression left me. I don't know exactly what happened except that Christ delivered me. I'm not a workaholic anymore but a much more mellow person. I don't have a girlfriend but I'm happy. And it's amazing to me that I'm so close to people who are Puerto Rican, Jamaican, African American, or whatever. After all, I'm an Italian guy who grew up in a neighborhood that had the usual kinds of prejudice toward minorities. But I don't have any of the poison in my heart since Christ changed me. Now I'm part of God's family and I love it."

I hadn't yet met Bob Adamo nor heard all the other stories of what God had done that night, but I knew that he was working. After the concert, I walked outside. Suddenly, a wolf pack of boys emerged from the subway, ready for trouble. As they passed me, one of them punched me in the back for no good reason and nearly knocked me to the street. At any other time, I would have been shocked by such an attack. But I was too drained from the physical and emotional strain of the concert to worry. Instead, I felt encouraged because I knew that someone was obviously displeased by what had taken place in one of the city's premier theaters. That little jolt from Satan couldn't begin to rob me of my joy.

MY PROVIDER

Every day I come into contact with people who appear to be supremely confident of themselves. That's especially true in a fast-paced environment like New York City, where it's been said that only the strong survive. Anyone who has lived here knows that unless you are assertive you're likely to be trampled. Weakness is never admired in any culture or society and is almost always equated with failure and inferiority. If you're weak, you are often taken advantage of or abused.

Christianity, however, is based on very different principles. The more you grow in God, the more you realize that he is calling you to be a living contradiction to the values of this world. God loves to see us acknowledge our weakness because that leads us to dependence on him. Our complete dependence gives God full reign to glorify himself without our feeble self-efforts getting in the way.

It's almost comical when you consider how foolish we must look when we proudly base our identities in our abilities. Do our abilities impress God? He simply spoke the world into existence. He's omnipresent, omnipotent, and omniscient—so how could I ever think that my ability to play the piano or write a song could somehow impress him?

The apostle Paul addresses the issue of self-confidence in his letter to the Philippians. Paul had a lot going for him by the standards of his world. To prove this he includes a long and impressive list of his credentials. What a surprise it is when he follows this by saying that he counts all of these things as loss that he might know Christ. Paul longed to know Jesus more than anything else in the world. He knew that no achievement, gifting, or ability could aid him in his pursuit. In fact, he understood that these very things had the potential of becoming a hindrance to knowing God if they gave him a sense of self-sufficiency.

In his second letter to the Corinthians Paul explains that God's power is made perfect in his weakness. He offers his experience as proof that the power of Christ actually "rests" on us when we are weak. When we acknowledge our limits we open ourselves to the unlimited grace of God.

This has been the story of my own life. Over and over, God has stretched me, asking me to serve him in ways I simply couldn't without his grace. In those times of my own weakness, I have watched God intervene in ways that only he can take credit for. God has faithfully proven that "when I am weak, then I am strong."

MORE THAN ENOUGH

If you were able to direct the choir some Sunday, you probably wouldn't believe what needs lie behind each smiling face. You wouldn't realize that you were looking at a young woman who has just been diagnosed with multiple sclerosis. You wouldn't know that the man in the front row has lost his job and has been unable to find another one. I doubt you would be able to spot the exhausted doctor who delivers babies day and night yet faithfully comes to choir practice and Sunday services. You would see so many others—the man laboring in prayer for his unsaved wife and the woman whose son is serving a life sentence for murder. If you knew all their stories, you might wonder how they are able to maintain the joy that is so evident on their faces. The answer can be found in the words of a song. It's called "More Than Enough," a song the choir sings with great conviction:

> Jehovah-Jireh, my provider
> > You are more than enough for me
> Jehovah Rapha, you're my healer
> > By your stripes I've been set free
> Jehovah Shammah, you are with me
> > You supply all my needs
> You are more than enough
> > More than enough, more than enough for me.

When I experience God providing for me in personal and tangible ways, it overwhelms me. His kindness is so hard to fathom. I begin to realize that God is fully able to protect and provide for me no matter how difficult my life may be.

But trust, I've learned, doesn't come naturally to most of us. It's something that develops not in the midst of good times but in the midst of difficult ones. The more we trust God no matter our current circumstances, the easier it will be to trust him for the future because we will see just how faithful he is towards us.

Whatever I know about trusting God first developed in my own family. I'm sure I absorbed it from parents who depended on God for everything, right down to the food they fed their six children. I can't talk about trust without telling you about them.

BEGINNINGS

My father, Clair Hutchins, grew up on a farm in Illinois, knowing little or nothing about God. His mother, Inez, was only eighteen when she married a thirty-eight-year-old widower with two sons who were nearly her own age. Then she gave birth to two sons, the second of which was my father. This unusual combination made for constant bickering and strife. It wasn't a happy home for a sweet-tempered boy to grow up in.

When Dad was in high school he entered a vocal contest and placed first in the state of Illinois. The prize was a scholarship to the American Conservatory of Music in Chicago. For a gentle man like my father, it was a relief to leave behind the contentiousness of his life at home. Later, when he left the conservatory, he joined the American Opera Company. It was the beginning of a promising career for the handsome young man with wavy brown hair. Anything could happen now. And something unexpected did.

One day, Dad decided to hitchhike home for a weekend on the farm. Standing on a dirt road outside of town, he was glad when a large sedan finally pulled over. Quickly he opened the passenger door, folding his lanky body into the front seat.

As the car bumped along the gravel road, the driver began talking. He spoke of a God who loves us more than any human being ever could. About a God so desperate to reveal himself that he became a man and was tortured and murdered by the people he loved. He talked about a God so powerful he raised his Son from the dead. The story captivated the attention of a young man unfamiliar with the gospel, and by the time he stepped out of the car and waved good-bye, my father's world had been turned upside down.

The driver of the car was none other than Dr. Robert Cook who later became the president of King's College, an evangelical school on the East Coast, and a well-known Bible teacher with a national radio program. Even though Dr. Cook had been driving a familiar route that day, he still managed to get lost. He never could figure out how he ended up on that Illinois back road, where Clair Hutchins stood waiting for a ride. However it happened, one man lost his way that day so another could find it. My dad was the first in his family to receive Jesus Christ as his Savior.

Dad was so overwhelmed by God's love that he put all his big plans on hold, ready to make whatever changes God might indicate. He decided to quit the opera company to attend Moody Bible Institute and later Northern Baptist Seminary. A few years before I was born, he accepted a position as music director for a church in Chicago and later as pastor of Beulah Temple, a church on the south side of Chicago.

When my father went out to preach on a Sunday morning, dressed in his navy blue suit, red tie, and white shirt, nobody looked better. A tall man who could make friends with anyone, he didn't care what color people were or where they came from or how much money they did or didn't make. He loved them all—especially his congregation—from the angriest old woman to the most overbearing member of the board of elders. But it wasn't easy for the rest of us to watch how he was sometimes treated by the people he tried to serve. No matter how unkind people were, he never retaliated. He never gave up on anyone. Dad was constantly preaching to me through his love.

Though I never felt poor, our family did go through some hard times. I remember one Christmas in particular. I was eight years old, living in Brooklyn. My dad made a small salary and out of that he had to support a wife and six children.

One Saturday just before Christmas he counted four dollar bills into my small hand and then took me to Woolworth's to do my Christmas shopping. Four dollars seemed like a lot to me until I tried to buy nine presents, seven for family members and two for my neighborhood playmates, Linda and Carol. Fortunately, I spotted two pair of anklets, one blue and one pink. Just perfect, I thought, for my friends.

I met my girlfriends on the street shortly before Christmas to exchange gifts. I went first, opening a beautifully wrapped box from Linda. Inside was my favorite board game. Then came Carol's gift to me, an expensive set of paper dolls. I was thrilled. Now it was my turn to hand over the presents I had so carefully selected for them. As soon as my little girlfriends opened their packages, they threw the socks in my face, grabbed the gifts they had given me, and ran straight home. So much for those friends.

I smile now, recalling the story. But I was devastated at the time. Despite such experiences, I felt my life was rich and full, surrounded by a large church family, five brothers and sisters, and parents who loved me. And of course there was that friend of my brother, Jimmy Cymbala, traipsing in and out of our house.

TRUSTING GOD TOGETHER

As time went on, my relationship with Jim Cymbala began to change. By the time I was fifteen, he no longer thought of me as a pesky little sister. And I no longer thought of him as someone who was merely my brother's best friend. Jim began writing to me from the U.S. Naval Academy, where he had been attending school. Like any couple we suffered our share of ups and downs over the years that followed. We'd argue, break up, and get back together. But during all that time, somehow neither of us doubted we would marry someday.

After I graduated from high school, I didn't go to college but worked at a couple of different jobs before taking a position as a receptionist at a pharmaceutical company. Meanwhile, Jim left the Naval Academy because of a back injury and completed his degree at the University of Rhode Island. Finally, he came home to Brooklyn, landing a good job with an airline company. Then, when I was twenty-one we got married and moved into a nice apartment in Brooklyn. Now that we were together, life should have been just about perfect. Instead, we felt miserable.

The problem was God.

What I mean is that God was trying to get our attention, but we weren't listening particularly well. Jim had been sensing God calling him into full-time ministry, but he just didn't feel qualified. After all, he had no credentials. He hadn't spent a single day in Bible school, let alone in seminary. He didn't know a word of Greek or Hebrew. What did he know about preaching or pastoring a church? Plus he had a wife and child to support. Our daughter, Chrissy, was born just eleven months after we married.

> *Now that Jim and I were together, life should have been just about perfect. Instead, we felt miserable.*

For my part, I was simply going along with things, trying to be a good wife. But neither of us felt comfortable just going to church on Sunday and leaving it at that. God was creating a restlessness in us that we couldn't manage to shake.

By then my father was no longer the pastor of a single church but was overseeing two congregations. One day he called Jim to say that the church in Newark needed a pastor, and my dad asked Jim if he would be willing to fill in. Jim said he'd pray about it. One day he came home from work, sat me down, and said, "Look, Carol, I resigned my job today. I just have to obey God. We need to start working in the church in Newark."

I didn't feel resentful that he hadn't consulted me before resigning because I knew this was what God wanted us to do.

I felt relieved that we were taking this step even though we didn't know where the money would come from.

ADJUSTING

And money wasn't the only issue. I was young, with a new baby, and my husband lacked formal training. On top of all that, this inner-city African-American congregation was made up of people mostly in their thirties and forties. This accented our youth and placed us in a unique cultural situation.

Still, this was not a new experience for either of us. I had grown up in my father's church in Brooklyn, and he had always accepted people regardless of their race. That fact, combined with white flight to the suburbs, had changed the church's racial composition so that by the time I was eleven years old, my church world was largely black. Jim, on the other hand, had been busy playing basketball in the color-blind playgrounds of New York City. The truth is that most of our lives, before and after our move to Newark, had been spent learning about other cultures.

Though I loved the variety that such experiences inevitably bring, I have been guilty of my share of blunders. Like the time I invited West Indian guests to share a Thanksgiving meal with our family. I remember laboring over the meal while I was eight months pregnant with my second child. It never occurred to me that our guests might prefer spicier food than the traditional American feast. The table was beautiful, the bird was golden, the mashed potatoes were a creamy white, smothered with gravy. But our guests just picked at their food, no doubt thinking it bland and rather strange. Our attempt at hospitality seemed like a complete disaster. I was so exhausted that night that after everyone left I just collapsed onto the couch and cried.

THE LITTLE CHURCH WITH BIG PROBLEMS

The church in Newark paid Jim a modest salary, and though we were young and inexperienced, the people in the congregation accepted us with relatively little difficulty. And Jim and I no longer felt restless. We were glad to be doing what we felt God wanted.

After we had been in Newark for two years, my father called Jim one day. He wanted to talk about a little church in Brooklyn that was having big troubles. Ironically, my mother was partially responsible for the situation. Years earlier she and a few friends had been praying for God to raise up a church where his power would be manifested. That was the beginning of the Brooklyn Tabernacle, which grew up on Atlantic Avenue right across the street from where they had been praying.

My father had been overseeing this tiny struggling church. Would Jim, he wondered, be willing to speak for four consecutive Sunday nights to help out the young pastor in downtown Brooklyn? Two weeks after Jim said yes, the pastor there resigned. He'd had enough. Still, Dad wasn't ready to give up on the church. So he asked Jim to pastor the church in Brooklyn in addition to the one he was already caring for in Newark. That meant racing back and forth between the two churches, wearing ourselves out in the process.

Sundays were a madhouse of activity with Jim going to Brooklyn from our home in New Jersey early in the morning to lead a Sunday worship service. He would then head back to Newark, where I was playing the organ for a noon service already in progress, and preach a sermon. After this we would jump in the car with our daughter Chrissy and head to McDonald's for our Sunday meal. Then we would make the drive back to downtown Brooklyn together for a Sunday evening service. After a couple of years of trying to care for both churches, we realized we had to make a choice. Either stay in Newark or move to the little church with big problems.

It would have been so easy to drop the church in Brooklyn. Nobody would have blamed us. But both Jim and I felt God tugging at our hearts to devote full-time service there even though our only real salary came from the church in New Jersey. To help pay the bills, I took a job in a school cafeteria while Jim worked as a junior high school basketball coach.

Most people would have thought us crazy for making the choice we did. But we never thought what we were doing was all that unusual. It didn't matter that we didn't know how we would support ourselves. It never crossed our minds to ask if this next step would further Jim's career path. What career path? We weren't worried about health insurance. Who had health insurance anyway? We were just trying to respond to God. Just trying to be faithful.

So we took the plunge and did exactly what we thought God wanted us to do and everything worked out beautifully. Right? Of course not!

Life in Brooklyn was nothing but difficult. We inherited a small congregation at odds with itself. Soon our group dwindled even more because some folks didn't like Jim's style compared to what was going on before. Only about twenty people would actually admit to being members. The building was as out of shape as the congregation. The basement reeked of mildew, the ceiling in the auditorium fell with a huge thud during a service one day, and a pew full of people collapsed in the sanctuary on a Sunday morning while Jim was preaching. I guess you could say it was the opposite of a standing ovation. Jim was so depressed that sometimes even he didn't want to go to church.

Because the church badly needed some kind of musical ministry, and because I played the keyboard and had a good ear for music, I formed a small choir. Though I was painfully timid, this was something I had always longed to do. But our small band of singers was nothing to brag about. On Friday nights I led practice while Jim took care of the kids. Saturdays were taken up with weddings or other church activities. During the service, I would sometimes sing the solos while playing the piano and directing the choir at the same time! I can't remember a single Sunday when I was able to sit with my children in church. And I was so desperate for choir members that I took anyone who applied, even if they were tone deaf. Consequently, we had every problem in the book.

It wasn't easy to trust God, especially during that first year when the choir had only nine members and one of the young men in the tenor section got one of the altos pregnant. Then one night a church member went berserk. She grabbed a knife, came into the practice, and went crazy, cutting up the drums and threatening everyone in sight. We had to forcibly restrain her, dragging her screaming from the room. Talk about a difficult choir practice!

> *The basement reeked of mildew, the ceiling in the auditorium fell with a huge thud during a service one day, and a pew full of people collapsed in the sanctuary on a Sunday morning while Jim was preaching. I guess you could say it was the opposite of a standing ovation.*

SIGNS OF DAYLIGHT

Neither Jim nor I could imagine what God might be doing in the midst of such sorry circumstances. Finally, when we had reached our lowest point, God began to make his intentions clear. It happened on a fishing boat off the coast of Florida one day. My folks had invited Jim to their home near the shore to recuperate from a hacking cough that had hung on for six weeks. With all the pressure he was under in New York, he badly needed the break. Though Jim didn't reel in any fish, he netted a far better catch that day, because that was when God spoke to him about what he wanted to do with our lives.

Jim tells the story in *Fresh Wind, Fresh Fire*. He was alone at the back of the boat, enjoying a quiet moment as he prayed about our situation.

> "Lord, I have no idea how to be a successful pastor.... I haven't been trained. All I know is that Carol and I are working in the middle of New York City, with people dying on every side, overdosing from heroin, consumed by materialism, and all the rest. If the gospel is so powerful ..."
>
> Then quietly but forcefully, in words heard not with my ear but deep within my spirit, I sensed God speaking:
>
> *If you and your wife will lead my people to pray and call upon my name, you will never lack for something fresh to preach. I will supply all the money that's needed, both for the church and for your family, and you will never have a building large enough to contain the crowds I will send in response.*
>
> I was overwhelmed.[1]

When Jim returned he told me what had happened, and we began to make prayer the primary focus of the church. We started a real prayer meeting on Tuesday nights, and as we prayed the church began to grow and old wounds began to heal. People started coming off the streets for prayer and

[1]Jim Cymbala, *Fresh Wind, Fresh Fire* (Grand Rapids: Zondervan, 1997), p. 25.

many joined the church. God gave us a wonderful sense of love and unity. It was like seeing the first signs of daylight after a very long night.

During the preceding years it had felt as though we were using all our energy to establish a foundation that kept crumbling beneath us. It would have been so easy to abandon the work, to stop trusting God because of all the obstacles we faced. Now the foundation was secure and the building had begun. It didn't matter that we still had a lot of hard work ahead of us. We could see the fruit of our labor and couldn't wait to move forward in God's plan.

The little church with big problems still had problems, but we began to see God solving them one by one as we cried out to him in prayer. Instead of a church on life support, the Brooklyn Tabernacle was being transformed into a spiritual emergency room, a place of rescue for those who felt crushed by the darkness around them, by the violence, addiction, harshness, and despair that characterized the city. God's medicine began to work wonders.

Before we knew it the choir had grown to fifty members. Since I didn't know how to read music, I would figure out the song arrangements in my head and teach them to the choir by rote. Later Teen Challenge asked us to cooperate with them on rallies they were holding in a large church in downtown

> *Instead of a church on life support, the Brooklyn Tabernacle was being transformed into a spiritual emergency room, a place of rescue for those who felt crushed by the darkness around them, by the violence, addiction, harshness, and despair that characterized the city. God's medicine began to work wonders.*

Brooklyn on Saturday nights. I formed another choir with the Teen Challenge guys, most of whom were ex-drug addicts and few of whom could sing on key.

From those rallies the church really started to grow. And I was growing too. No longer feeling so out of my depth, sure that God was in our midst and that he was providing everything we needed to remain faithful to the work he had given us. One thing I knew for certain: Jim and I could not possibly survive in Brooklyn if God had not called us to be there. The work would devour us. But God wasn't about to let the darkness swallow up what he had started.

GOD IS WORKING

I wish you could come with me to the Wall Street station in downtown Manhattan on a Friday morning, just in time to watch the subway trains roll into the heart of the financial district. At first, the station seems empty, with hardly a soul in sight. Jokingly called "cattle cars," trains soon arrive, each carrying its cargo of stockbrokers, lawyers, and white- and blue-collar workers, all on their way to downtown jobs. As the doors slide open hundreds of commuters spill out, creating a massive human traffic jam as they push their way up the stairways on their way to work.

Now come with me to the station on a weekend morning at exactly the same time. It's an entirely different scene. The trains roll in right on time but hardly anyone gets out. For most people this is a Monday-to-Friday, nine-to-five kind of stop.

Now think for a moment about a person who never stops working. This person is not a workaholic but never needs a break. He works night and day, year in year out, never taking a holiday. Better yet, he is always working on your behalf. Even while you sleep, even when you are too sick to make it into the office, God is working.

Though we know that God is always working in the world, we are sometimes tempted to doubt that he is truly concerned about our own lives. Where is he, we sometimes wonder, when we need him the most? Because his work is invisible, we cannot rely on our natural vision to keep us during hard times. Without faith, we may think that God doesn't know what's happening or that he doesn't care. And that is why the apostle Paul says, "We live by faith, not by sight" (2 Corinthians 5:7).

The title song of the choir's latest album is "God Is Working." The lyrics reaffirm the fact that our God is at work behind the scenes of life:

God is working, He's still working
God is working even now.
Though we often don't know just how
God is working even now.
Though you cannot see and you can't quite understand,
Remember God is still in control.
He has promised to bring you through somehow
And He's working even now.

> By reminding myself of how God has worked, I find it easier to believe that he is still working.

Whenever I am tempted to wonder where God is during some crisis in my life, I just remember his Word and all the ways he has already worked in demonstrating his power to me. By reminding myself of how God *has* worked, I find it easier to believe that he *is still* working. For me, the key to faith in hard times is remembering God's promises, counting on him to be the one he says he is who will do what he says he will.

TIME TO SURRENDER

Some of my memories of how God has worked on my behalf take me back to a farm in southern Wisconsin. My mother,

Wilma Arn, was born there in 1918. Her parents were hard working Swiss immigrants who were doing their best to launch their fourteen children into the world. My mother was seventh in the lineup.

Small, dark haired, and determined, Mom was only sixteen when she packed up and moved to Chicago to attend beauty school. To make ends meet she worked for a dentist and his wife, cleaning and helping out with chores around the house. There wasn't anything she wouldn't attempt, like making a table full of banana crème pies for a bar mitzvah, for instance.

In a day when few women worked outside of the home and there were few small business loans for women entrepreneurs, Mom succeeded in opening her own beauty shop and running it like a pro.

After work, she used to frequent a little coffee shop in the neighborhood. One evening, when she was twenty-one, a good-looking young guy approached her as she sat at the counter eating dinner. His line was a familiar one, but it worked well enough: "Excuse me, miss. Would you happen to know the time?" The two struck up a conversation, and in the weeks that followed kept bumping into each other at the coffee shop, each one hoping the other would be there.

Neither of them were Christians. But when Mom took him home to meet the family, a strange thing happened. Her mother, my grandma Arn, was a woman of great prayer and unusual discernment. Before they parted, Grandma looked her future son-in-law in the eye and told him boldly: "You're going to be in the ministry one day." Though Mom may have been surprised, she wasn't alarmed. She felt safe in the knowledge that this young man, Clair Hutchins, was no more religious than she.

At the time my parents married, my father was still with the American Opera Company. But after his encounter with

Dr. Robert Cook, things changed. The more Dad talked about Jesus, the more resistant Mom became. She wanted to live her life the way she wanted to live it, and Jesus was definitely not part of the plan. She had married an opera singer, not a minister. And she wanted to keep it that way.

One day as she was cleaning house, she began to feel as though someone else was in the room speaking to her. It wasn't an audible voice but an impression so strong she couldn't get rid of it. *This is the day of salvation,* the voice said. The words shook her so much that she ran out the door and down the street, with the vacuum still running. Then, at the end of the street she broke down. In broad daylight, on a quiet side street in the heart of Chicago, she began to sob. God wanted her life and she began to surrender it at that moment. No more running, no more evading.

Back in Wisconsin, a mother on her knees was getting one more prayer answered.

GOD'S HEALING WORK

God has allowed me to experience different challenges throughout my life, which have been used to prove the power of prayer. By the time I was born in December 1947, my father had already accepted a call to become the pastor of Beulah Temple and Mom was his biggest supporter. Then when I was four years old, Mom became pregnant with her fourth child. The pregnancy went well at first. But in a few months she became so ill that she couldn't get out of bed. No one realized she had developed toxemia and that the baby inside her had been dead for several weeks. Finally my mother lapsed into a coma. I can still remember the night the ambulance came for her, can still hear the strange rattling noise in her throat as they rolled her away on the stretcher.

My mother delivered the baby shortly after she was admitted to the hospital. After that her body began to mend but during the following years she suffered from periodic seizures that would rob her of her memory and weaken her considerably. And there was no telling when they would hit. Sometimes I would come home from school and find her in the middle of a horrible seizure. Mom would emerge from these episodes so dazed that she couldn't tell you her name let alone the names of her six children. After a few days, normalcy would return, but we knew it wouldn't be long until she suffered another seizure.

Years later, a dear friend and prayer partner came over to the house after one of my mother's attacks. This was a woman who was blessed with a kind of immovable faith. "Listen, kids," she told us, "your mother and I are going upstairs, and we are going to shut the door and pray. Don't worry if we don't come down for a while, because we are not coming out until she is healed."

So Mom and her friend stayed in that room all day and all night. Then another day and night and another day after that. For three days, they didn't eat a thing as strong cries and petitions went up to heaven. Finally, Mom opened the door and walked out. She never suffered another seizure in her life.

Seeing such a dramatic change in someone you love can't help but shape your understanding of God's power and your sense that he is capable of anything. It was a good thing, because when I reached third grade, I was the one who needed a miracle. By the time I was diagnosed with rheumatic fever, the doctor, rather unprofessionally, told my parents that my heart had turned to mush. He said it had already been so badly damaged that I would need to stay in bed for the next year and a half. I wasn't even allowed to walk to the bathroom. Nurses buzzed in and out of the room day after day drawing blood while the doctor made a house call once a week to see if my heart was still beating. I wasn't expected to live.

But the church prayed for me and kept praying. After some months in bed, my body began to heal. Finally, I was strong enough to return to school and carry on with my life. God had healed me in just a few months time. Still, the rheumatic fever had lingering effects. I never played the way other children did. Never joined in a lot of physical activity. Most of my time was spent indoors sitting on a bench playing the piano. I was captivated by music, especially beautiful chord progressions and unusual harmonies from songs I'd heard.

Seeing such a dramatic change in someone you love can't help but shape your understanding of God's power and your sense that he is capable of anything. It was a good thing, because when I reached third grade, I was the one who needed a miracle.

My sense of God's power was not limited to the healings my mother and I experienced. My youngest brother, Perry, was born with spinal meningitis. The doctors didn't think he would live either. If he did manage to survive, they said, he would never rise above a vegetative state. Of course the doctors lacked one vital piece of information when they made their diagnosis. They didn't realize they were dealing with a family that believed in the power of God.

Despite the situation, my father came to the hospital one day followed by a parade of elders from the church. The men huddled around my brother's crib, anointed him with oil, and prayed with all their hearts. And God was merciful. My brother was completely healed.

After that, no one could tell me that God was some kind of distant being, rarely involved in our lives. I knew he wasn't simply standing back, watching us like a detached observer. Instead, he was powerfully involved in my life and the lives of those around me.

GOD IS STILL WORKING

And God hasn't stopped working in our lives. My mother is eighty-two years old. Last year she was diagnosed with stomach cancer. When I flew down to Florida to visit her, I was shocked to see how pale she looked. My once vigorous mother seemed to be slipping away in front of my eyes. Finally, my sister and I called an ambulance, fearing the worst.

We soon discovered that Mom had been bleeding internally. After she regained a little of her strength, I returned to New York. Mom was scheduled to have surgery on a Friday, and I'll never forget the call I got from my brother-in-law just before I walked into choir practice that night. "Carol, it looks really bad. They had to remove about two-thirds of her stomach and the doctor pulled me aside after surgery and told me to call hospice. He says she only has about three months to live and we should be sure she has a living will."

I wanted to cry, to break down sobbing. But I couldn't. It was nearly time to teach the choir a new song I had written, "Nothing Is Impossible." I'd written the words a few months earlier, never thinking I would have to hold them in my heart on my mother's behalf:

> Nothing, nothing at all, nothing, nothing at all
> Is impossible, impossible with God.
> It is no secret what God can do.
> What He's done for others, He can still do for you.
> There's nothing impossible, impossible with God.
> There is no doubting, there is no fear.
> Just put your trust in Jesus and the answer is near.
> There's nothing impossible, impossible with God.
> When He speaks you know it's done.
> Through Jesus Christ his Son
> There is nothing impossible, impossible with God.

We walk by faith, never by sight.
Our faith is in Christ Jesus, through the power of His
    might.
There's nothing impossible, impossible with God.
Jesus is listening,
He hears your prayer.
Shake off discouragement and give Him your cares.
There's nothing impossible, impossible with God.

As the choir sang the song over and over, learning it by rote, the lyrics sank into my own heart, increasing my faith about my mother's situation.

When Dad died a few years ago, I knew it was his time. He was a tired soldier who just wanted to go home. But I really didn't think it was Mom's time to go. I was full of faith that God still had a work he wanted to do in and through her.

I flew back down to Florida to see how she was doing after surgery. When I walked into her hospital room I noticed a beautiful bouquet of roses standing on the ledge. I had never seen roses like that in my life. They were so huge and thick, so full of life. "Ma," I said. "Look at those roses, they represent life. You're not going to die. It doesn't matter what the doctors say. Right there is another confirmation that God wants you to live." It wasn't just wishful thinking on my part. I could feel faith rising inside me. I was absolutely confident that God was working to heal my mother.

> It wasn't just wishful thinking on my part. I could feel faith rising inside me. I was absolutely confident that God was working to heal my mother.

Shortly after the operation she was out and about eating tacos and pizza. Mom felt great. Apparently no one had told her stomach that most of it had been removed.

Today, eighteen months later, my mother is back in her own home, cooking for her grandchildren, driving a car. Remarkably, her doctors have now given her a clean bill of health. And I believe God has given her added years to continue her ministry of intercessory prayer.

Remembering how God has worked in my life helps to strengthen my faith for the present and gives me greater hope for the future. As I look back I start to realize that God was at work long before I was born, in the lives of my parents and grandparents, to shape the work he is doing today. Many of us have heard it for so long that it sounds trite to say that God has a plan for our lives. But he does. And the difficult circumstances of our lives never thwart his plan.

My father was a minister. My husband's father was an alcoholic. Maybe your father was a millionaire or a drug addict. Whatever your story, whether your life has been easy or hard, God has a plan for your life and he will continue to work it out as you open your heart to him.

If the Brooklyn Tabernacle leaves a legacy of any sort, I believe it will be the story of how God has worked to change the lives of so many broken people. When you see how God works day after day, it's impossible to be cynical or to put limits on his power. We have people in the church who are former drug dealers, prostitutes, alcoholics, and thieves. We have "respectable" people who nearly destroyed themselves in their pursuit of pleasure. Others lived empty lives although their bank accounts were full. We have blacks who used to hate whites and whites who used to hate blacks. We have both victims and abusers. Though I'm no longer shocked by the stories I hear, I still stand in awe when I think of the powerful ways God works to bring all kinds of people to himself.

JOSH'S STORY

Josh Carroll, who is now a tenor in the choir, was once a young man who was living according to plan. But it wasn't a plan God had put in motion. It started long before he was born.

"My grandfather died after his heart had been weakened from years of drinking and smoking. My other grandfather was an alcoholic too. I started drinking when I was fourteen. By the time I was seventeen I was a drunk.

"There's not a lot to do in Nebraska, so every night my girlfriend and I would drive around in the cornfields, drinking and listening to music. One night at a party I drank so much beer and smoked so much pot that when we got into the car to leave, I saw three of her. Though it was snowing and the roads were slick, I managed to get her home safely. But I was so drunk I couldn't find my way home though I lived just five minutes away. After stopping at a phone booth to call a friend for directions to my own house, I climbed back behind the wheel and then nodded off. The car veered off the road and slammed into a ditch. I woke up when my head hit the steering wheel. When I got out of the car, the first thing I noticed was a large white cross straight ahead of me. Ironically, I had landed directly across from the church I'd grown up in. As I turned around and looked at the path my tires had plowed through the snow, I realized the car had barely squeaked between a fire hydrant and a light pole, to the left and right of which were large drop-offs. A slightly larger car wouldn't have made it through.

"I looked back again at the cross. 'Thank you, God, for saving my life,' I prayed. That night, I knew someone was trying to get my attention. Problem was my attention kept wandering.

"By then my parents had become really concerned about me. But nothing they said made any difference. I knew they had always prayed for me but I didn't know that they had redoubled their prayers when they saw the direction my life was taking. They didn't want to see me end up like my two grandfathers had.

"The next year I celebrated Christmas night in jail. I had been arrested for drunk driving. When my dad bailed me out, he broke down: 'Josh, when we got your call last night, your mother and I thought it was the morgue telling us to come and pick up your body. You really scared us last night.' My parents had prayed for me and with me. I knew they wanted me to change my life and live for God.

I looked back again at the cross. "Thank you, God, for saving my life," I prayed. That night, I knew someone was trying to get my attention. Problem was my attention kept wandering.

"But instead of listening I packed my bags and moved to New York to pursue an acting career. Acting was my one ambition. I'd gotten a taste for the stage by playing roles in community and high school plays ever since I was thirteen. But once in New York, I was so lonely I spent most nights in my apartment guzzling a twelve-pack of beer. After a while I got used to attending auditions with a hangover. That's how I met Marleen, standing in line to try out for a musical review that was going to be staged at a resort in Wisconsin.

"She had long white-blonde hair and was so attractive I figured she wouldn't give me a second look. But we started talking, and I found out she had come to New York just three days before I had. Like me she was lonely, mixed up, and messed up, though I didn't know it at first. We were a perfect match.

"Marleen and I started seeing each other and were both hired for the job in Wisconsin. It was good money, and we only had to work a couple of hours a day, so I spent the rest of my time drinking. Marleen drank but not as much as I did. Once she dared me to go for a week without a drink. Impossible! I didn't even last two days. Any girl in her right mind would have dumped me right then.

Like me she was lonely, mixed up, and messed up, though I didn't know it at first. We were a perfect match.

"One day, someone let me in on a secret. A number of people from the cast had been breaking into the bar of the resort and stealing beer. Great, I thought. No need to stop partying when the bars close down. So I started stealing as well. But somebody tipped off the police, and I got caught. I was booked for burglary and thrown into jail. Marleen was arrested too, though she hadn't been involved.

"Here we were stuck in a little town in Wisconsin charged with a felony offense. We didn't know anyone except the people we worked with, and we'd just been fired. I was in such a daze that I flopped down on the cot in my cell and didn't move a muscle for seven straight hours. Finally, I began to pray. 'God I don't know what to do and I don't know if you even care about me anymore. I've passed up every opportunity you've given me . . . but please help me this time.' I was so scared.

"Suddenly I felt as if I wasn't alone. I knew the presence of God was in my cell right then, and I promised him that if he would get me out of this mess I would do anything he wanted. The next morning they handcuffed me to another prisoner, and I walked into a room where I saw Marleen, locked to another female prisoner. Finally they released us, warning us not to leave town before our court date.

"My dad arrived the next night and took us out to dinner. He was disappointed, but very understanding. He knew Marleen didn't grow up knowing a lot about Jesus. So he prayed with us and encouraged us to look to God for help.

"One night he sat me down: 'Josh, you don't have any idea how much the Lord loves you and what lengths he will go to in order to show you that you need him.' Dad wouldn't let up. His words kept droning in my ear, piercing me, giving me a headache. As he talked I felt the Lord dealing with me again. But it wasn't a peaceful feeling. Instead, I felt troubled, like something inside me was all churned up.

"Dad stayed until the day of our hearing. We were pretty sure Marleen would get off with a fine, but it seemed certain I would get two or three years in prison. Before we went into court Dad told me he had been praying that morning and had felt the Lord assure him everything would turn out alright. God didn't want me to rot in prison, but he did want to get my attention. He had it.

"I was amazed when the DA let Marleen and me off with a $400 fine. That was it. Just leave the state and don't come back.

"So the two of us flew back to New York. Though I didn't forget what had happened in that jail cell, I still wasn't ready to admit how much I needed God. As soon as we got back, Marleen and I

> *Dad wouldn't let up. His words kept droning in my ear, piercing me, giving me a headache. As he talked I felt the Lord dealing with me again. But it wasn't a peaceful feeling. Instead, I felt troubled, like something inside me was all churned up.*

moved in together, but the more we were together, the more we fought. Pretty soon we didn't even like each other. I guess misery was the glue that kept us together.

"Finally, someone handed Marleen a flyer about the Brooklyn Tabernacle, and we decided we might as well go. We were so desperate. On Sunday we fought all the way to church, yelling at each other as we walked down the streets of Brooklyn. I was in a rage as I walked through the door of the church. But once inside I felt a kind of peace. And I calmed right down.

"After that, we decided to go to the Tuesday night prayer meeting as well. Again we argued all the way. But as people began praying, I started weeping. God's presence was so strong, and all I could think of was how much I had sinned against him. I started telling God that I didn't know what to do about my life. I told him how much I hated myself. I hated the way I treated Marleen. I hated the drinking. I hated the fact that I was afraid to go to sleep at night without the lights and the television on.

When I woke the next morning it wasn't with a hangover, but with a sense that I was no longer alone. God was right beside me. He was like a medicine to me.

"And then I sensed God soothing me, telling me it was all right. He didn't care what I had done. He loved me. He always had. He wanted me to know him. Nothing else mattered.

"I'm not ashamed to say I fell in love with Jesus that night.

"God cleaned up my life immediately. As soon as Marleen and I got home, I told her I was going to start sleeping on the couch. I stopped drinking right away and stopped cursing too. I used to want so many things: to be a star, to make it big, and to have people admire me. Now these desires seemed ridiculous. When I woke the next morning it wasn't with a hangover, but with a sense that I was no longer alone. God was right beside me. He was like a medicine to me.

"God has done so much that it's hard to express how deep the changes go. I'm a member of the choir now and am no longer pursuing an acting career. And I'm happy about it. God has done a lot in Marleen as well, drawing her to himself. Together we were a sloppy mess. But we were perfect for the Lord."

No mess, no matter how long it's taken to make, is too much for the Lord to clean up. Jesus didn't come for those who have it all together but for those who are willing to admit their lives are worthless without him. If you met Josh Carroll today you would see a young man filled with God's peace. You would never guess about his struggles with alcoholism. I can imagine what it must have been like for Josh's parents watching him as he was destroying himself. The more they prayed, the worse things got. If they had only seen with their eyes, they would have thought God was paying absolutely no attention to their son. But they didn't. Instead they prayed harder, believing God was still at work even though they couldn't see the slightest bit of evidence that he was. And they were right. God was working, using the darkest things in Josh's life to make an opening for his light.

Maybe you have been spending a lot of time on your knees lately on behalf of a son or a daughter who is as troubled as Josh was. You've begged God to help them but you haven't seen any results. I've been there myself and I know that heartbreak. Or perhaps you've called out to God about a situation in your life that's caused you deep pain. I want to encourage you to consider the stories I've told you about how the Lord has worked in my own family and Josh's as evidence, not of special treatment but of special love. It's the love God has for all of us. So keep praying. Don't stop trusting. Even though you can't see it with your natural eyes, by faith you can know that God is working even now.

WHERE EVERYTHING BEGINS

Sometimes the greatest answers to prayer happen when you have no place to go but God. In the early 1970s, the Brooklyn Tabernacle was located in a rundown building on Atlantic Avenue in downtown Brooklyn. As the church began to grow, we rented additional space in a local branch of the YWCA, which we soon outgrew. One day, Jim spotted a "for sale" sign on a large theater on Flatbush Avenue. Able to seat 1,500 people, it seemed like a perfect place for God's work to grow.

The only problem was the one we've always had—no money. Still, after praying about it, we believed the Lord wanted the theater to become our new church. So Jim acted on his faith by signing a contract to purchase it despite the fact that we didn't have the money to buy it. The only way to make good on the contract would be to sell our run-down wreck of a building. But who would pay good money for a place like ours, we wondered?

Then, within days, a local pastor approached us to express interest in buying the property. He was willing to pay the asking price—just what we needed to make good on our contract for the theater. We couldn't believe how easy the whole process was. It looked like our troubles were solved. Then, after an entire month had passed, we discovered that the pastor was in even worse financial shape than we were. By now, our contract to buy the theater was running out. If God didn't do something soon, we would lose the building.

So Jim explained the situation to the congregation at the next Tuesday night prayer meeting. He began by telling them the good news: we had found the perfect building for our growing church. Then the challenging news: we didn't have the money for it unless God intervened powerfully on our behalf. That night, all of us, from the youngest to the oldest member of the church, literally cried out to God. One man prayed so earnestly that his tears formed a puddle on the carpet by his knees.

The next morning, the doorbell rang. Standing on the stoop was a Middle Eastern business man who inquired whether the building was still for sale. Jim was almost too embarrassed to tell him the asking price. But instead of laughing or politely excusing himself, the man simply asked to tour the building. As he led the man through the church, Jim kept noticing one thing after another that was falling apart. How, he wondered, could anyone even look twice at a building like this?

After the tour, the man asked the price again. Jim swallowed hard and repeated the figure. Suddenly, the man stuck out his hand and said, "I want to buy your building."

"But you'll have to go to a bank, and they'll have to approve you. And I don't even know who you are," Jim blurted out. He began thinking of all the possible delays and obstacles facing us. Even if this man could arrange financing it would still be too late to buy the theater because we wouldn't have the money in time.

"What bank? What mortgage?" the man answered. "This is a cash deal. Here is my lawyer's number. Have your lawyer call him, and I will buy your building."

That was it. When Jim came home that night and told me the story I almost fainted. The possibility of something like this happening seemed like one in a million. After just a few weeks, without using a realtor, we sold our decrepit building for an unheard of price and then used the money to purchase the theater. It's been our home for more than twenty years, a place where thousands of people have given their lives to Christ.

The evidence of God's faithfulness in our lives has been so real that neither Jim nor I have been tempted to explain away his promises. We're still counting on his Word to mean exactly what it says, because he continues to place us in situations where we have no choice but to rely on him as our prayer-answering God.

When you listen to the way God has worked in our lives, you may be tempted to think we're in some kind of special category. But Jim and I are no different than anyone else. The truth is that none of us can make it without the kind of help that comes through fervent prayer that touches the heart of God. Remember, too, that God makes us stronger as we persevere in prayer. It's never his will that we weaken and fall away from him. Whenever you think you can't go on for one more minute, pray and then keep praying. God will lift the load no matter what kind of pressure or challenge you may be facing. I know this is true because it's happened to me whenever I've been tempted to give up. God has always sustained me as I've poured out my heart to him in prayer.

THE SECRET OF SPIRITUAL STRENGTH

My maternal grandmother, Marie Arn, was a woman who wouldn't let anything or anybody stop her from praying. Not even her fourteen children. Not even an ungodly husband. No matter what was going on around her, she would often be on her knees for two and three hours a day, sometimes praying all night long. She was a woman whose spiritual discernment was right on the mark, shaped as it was by her prayer life. I believe her devotion to prayer is what gave her the strength to survive her difficult marriage and rear fourteen children in the process.

Communion with God was the great secret of her spiritual strength.

My grandmother lived on a farm outside the small town of Monticello, Wisconsin, which had a population of 792. She was still a young woman when a red-haired Assembly of God evangelist by the name of George Price set up a tent meeting in town one day. Determined to spread the gospel wherever they went, he and his wife carried everything they owned in a beat-up old car. No doubt their presentation was unpolished. But God was with them and they made six converts in this small town. One of them was my grandmother.

As determined as she was to live for God, her husband was determined not to. My grandfather wasn't happy about having a wife who spent the least bit of time or money on the church. In fact, he was so hostile to the gospel that he burned one of my grandmother's Bibles and once angrily locked her out of the house in the middle of winter when she went to church. But the more opposition she encountered, the more she persevered. She developed a rock solid faith in God that wouldn't be moved and even gained strength from the opposition she faced. If that was the cost of serving Jesus, she was more than willing to pay the price.

I don't know that my grandfather ever completely changed his mind about Christianity, but I think her patience and prayers helped soften him. For years, Grandma would ask for money to put in the offering plate, but he would always refuse. But as Grandpa got older, he began opening his wallet without being asked. He did it every Sunday.

It's no wonder that my grandmother felt her need for God so keenly. She must have known that her spiritual life depended on constant communion with God. Given her faith in God's promises, Grandma prayed right through every trial and tribulation that came her way. She learned through personal experience that prayer is powerful because it directly connects us to a powerful God who hears and answers.

My own mother was a wonderful example to me as well. As my father's ministry grew, he spent more time on the mission field and was often away on overseas trips. Even though he didn't have a church supporting him at the time, both my parents were convinced he was called to this work. Still there were six children to feed and clothe. I can remember my mother praying and fasting once for two weeks during one of Dad's many trips, asking God to help us. Shortly after that a wealthy businessman contacted us and offered to support Dad's missionary work on an ongoing basis.

> *In fact, my grandfather was so hostile to the gospel that he burned one of my grandmother's Bibles and once angrily locked her out of the house in the middle of winter when she went to church.*

In one of his letters to the early Christians, the apostle Paul remarked about the sincere faith of a mother and grandmother. These were women who passed their faith on to their son and grandson, Timothy, a young man who became Paul's disciple. Like Timothy I have been blessed since infancy with the godly examples of two generations of intercessors in my family.

Truthfully, I can't remember a time when I didn't pray. It isn't that I've always prayed as I should, but calling on God has become absolutely vital to me. It's only natural then, that

Given her faith in God's promises, I don't think Grandma ever made the mistake of throwing up her hands and complaining: "All I can do is pray," as though prayer was the least and weakest thing she could do in the face of trial and difficulties. She learned through personal experience that prayer is powerful because it directly connects us to a powerful God who hears and answers.

prayer would be at the heart of the ministry of the Brooklyn Tabernacle Choir.

THE PRAYER BEHIND THE PRACTICE

Several years ago Jerry Evans of J & J Music, the largest distributor of choral music in the country, and a good friend to Jim and me, came to me one day and asked: "Carol, what's your formula?"

I was so taken aback by Jerry's question that I just blurted out: "Jerry, there's no formula, we just pray, practice, and go out and sing. I guess it's as simple as that."

Every Friday night is choir practice and every practice begins with a time of prayer. We start praying at 6:30 P.M. and then gradually move into the rehearsal. Our time together usually ends around 10:00 P.M. or later if we are involved in a special project. Many nights, as I look out at the choir, I see brothers and sisters who seem spiritually battered and tired, just from dealing with life in New York City. As we turn to the Lord in prayer, I can see their burdens lifting. Because we spend this time with God, the Friday night practice has become a real oasis in a chaotic week. It's when we invite the Holy Spirit to fill us again so we can get up on Sunday and sing in a way that leads people into a deeply personal encounter with God.

So we pray as if we've never sung a song before, never won an award. Because we know that if God doesn't bless us, we won't be able to effectively minister to the people. And gospel music should never merely entertain. That cheapens it. God has given it to us so that lives can be changed. If that doesn't happen, what's the sense of singing? We know, too, that the deepest worship happens not when we raise our hands and shout "Alleluia" or sing a hand-clapping chorus. That's easy. The deepest worship happens as we surrender ourselves over and over to God. Jesus, while on earth, was the perfect example of this kind of worship.

> Sacrifice and offering you did not desire,
>   but a body you prepared for me;
> with burnt offerings and sin offerings
>   you were not pleased.
> Then I said, "Here I am—it is written about me
>   in the scroll—
>   I have come to do your will, O God."
>
> HEBREWS 10:5–7

When Jesus was baptized by John in the Jordan River, he showed his desire to do his Father's will. God was so pleased by his Son's humble submission that he expressed his approval for all to hear: "At that moment heaven was opened, and he [Jesus] saw the Spirit of God descending like a dove and lighting on him. And a voice from heaven said, 'This is my Son, whom I love; with him I am well pleased'" (Matthew 3:16–17). Our desire to do God's will opens heaven itself, and that's when we experience the Lord in all of his fullness.

I remember one of Jim's trips to Lima, Peru. He told me about a young couple he had met there who were being sent out to plant a church in a jungle area. They were headed to a place that had no church building, no congregation, and no

*We know, too,
that the deepest
worship happens
not when we raise
our hands and
shout "Alleluia" or
sing a hand-
clapping chorus.
That's easy.
The deepest worship
happens as we
surrender ourselves
over and over
to God.*

house to live in once they got there. Though they had little or no money, they had faith. As the church prayed over that young couple, the sense of God's presence was so strong that it overwhelmed everyone who was there that day. The sacrifice of a totally yielded life is the highest worship we can ever offer to God.

Joanne Brown, a soloist with the choir, talks about her experience during one of our Friday night prayer times:

"I always come early on Friday nights because if I miss the prayer—and I never do—then I miss the best part of being in the choir. We are so consumed by the presence of God that we some-times lose track of time and end our rehearsal without ever practicing. Carol usually begins by sharing something from the Word of God and then she leads us into a time of seeking God.

"I remember a time, not long ago, when I heard a sister weeping behind me as we prayed. I didn't know anything about what she might be going through but felt impressed to pray with her. A couple of other women joined me, and we began praying. I started asking God to heal her even though I had no idea if she was having any problems. Afterwards she said that her doctor had told her she might be suffering from lupus. That's why she'd been crying. When I prayed for her health, she knew that God was touching her, telling her he cared about what was going on in her life and that he was in control."

So often during our Friday night prayer times God works to bring us to the place of repentance for things he wants to change in our lives. During these times we experience his love, joy, and power so that we can serve others better. When we stand before a packed audience our confidence is in him as we minister the gospel through song.

I've told how God has worked in the lives of my mother and my grandmother, but every time I look out at the choir, I realize that every face there holds a story. Though these stories have taken shape in far different cultural settings than those of my grandmother and my mother, it is the same God who is still at work, still breaking and drawing people to himself. Let me tell you what I see when I look at Pam.

"GIVE ME SOMETHING REAL"

Pam Pettway has been a member of the choir for eight years. Before that she was a rap artist who recorded with Virgin Records. Pam was on the verge of becoming a hip-hop star, but God had something else in mind for her life.

"I was born on Father's Day in 1966. I guess it was appropriate because no child was prouder of her father than I was, especially every Sunday when he took me to the church where he served as an associate pastor. And my mother made me proud as well. With a bachelor's degree in theology, she was better equipped than most to be a leader's wife. My parents were my role models during my childhood. Along with my younger sister, we spent most of our free time in church, and the people there were like family.

"But the world fell apart when I was fifteen. That's when I learned that my dad had fallen into some problems and could not continue serving in the church. Soon after that, my parents divorced and Mom stopped taking us to our regular church. Because of that, we felt so cut off, so alienated from everyone we had always loved. I never understood why the people at that church, who had seemed like family, had dropped out of our lives so suddenly.

"Not only were we cut off from friends, but we also had very little money to live on. Before my parents divorced, we had everything we needed. Now we were hardly getting by. We were evicted from our apartment two different times because we couldn't pay the rent. One place was so shabby that mice ran around the living room. I remember how helpless and confused I felt. Nobody was the same. Not my mother. Not my sister. And especially not me. Everything was crazy, and I felt like I was having a nervous breakdown.

"Where was God in the midst of all this? Does he really see me? I wondered. *Does he even know I am here? Does he understand what I'm going through?* I felt so disappointed, so hopeless. It seemed like God had left us just like everyone else had.

"Whatever faith I had slowly faded, and I determined I would take my life into my own hands. Meanwhile, my sister married a man who became a big success in urban rap and hip-hop music. The head of Boogie Down Productions, my brother-in-law recorded several albums under the name KRS-One. His nickname at the height of his fame during the 1980s was 'The Teacher' because his raps were so politically and socially conscious. One of his records even went gold.

"In the late eighties, he got me a big recording contract with Virgin Records, who planned to break me into the music scene as a rapper who could sing. I was known as a positive rapper because my message wasn't about street violence but about God, family, and community. But I was talking about God apart from God, as though I were searching for him through my music. The record company didn't know what to do with a rapper who sang about God. I didn't fit in.

"At the same time I was doing a lot of speaking at various public schools in New York. Governor Mario Cuomo had earmarked funds to pay people like me to give pep talks as part of a drug prevention program. I'd talk to the kids, assuring them that they too could become a success if they just worked hard enough. Then I'd pocket the $100 I'd been paid for the talk and give the same spiel at the next school. I guess it was supposed to be good publicity for my career, but it was all so phony.

"The woman who drove me around to these speaking engagements happened to belong to the Brooklyn Tabernacle, and she kept urging me to visit the church. She didn't know I'd attended when I was seventeen and eighteen, without much enthusiasm. *Been there, done that,* I thought.

"Though I made a successful first recording and MTV aired my music video, Virgin Records still couldn't figure out what to do with me. It wasn't as though my career crashed and burned. It just fizzled.

"After that I felt so alone, so cold, living by myself in an expensive apartment in Brooklyn. Some nights I'd cross the street to a Japanese restaurant and order sushi and a bottle of beer. Then I'd carry it back to my apartment and eat it all by myself. But loneliness wasn't my only problem. I was running out of money too. Though the record company had paid me a large advance, I had nothing to show for it.

"One night, I broke down: 'Oh, God, if you are there, you have to help me. You have to show yourself to me because I don't understand life.' I felt I had no future, nothing left to hope for. I thought about killing myself.

"It wasn't as though I had nobody to lean on. By then, my relationship with both my parents was in good shape. I knew they were praying for me. I had friends. But I felt a kind of torment inside me that no one else knew about. It was easy to hide it by pretending everything was fine. Nobody knew what was really going on with me.

"Finally I gave in and went to the Brooklyn Tabernacle one Sunday. As I sat in the balcony and listened to the songs, I kept saying to myself: 'I've heard it all before but what does it really mean? How is it going to set me free? What is this peace, this love, this everlasting life that everybody talks about? Where is the "joy unspeakable and full of glory?" What is all this stuff about "He walks with me and he talks with me?"'

"I didn't want to be a churchgoer, who just goes through the motions. I'd had it with all the phoniness. I was so frustrated I felt like shouting: 'Give me something real or I am leaving. Give me Jesus or I am going to blow up!'

I didn't want to be a churchgoer, who just goes through the motions. I'd had it with all the phoniness. I was so frustrated I felt like shouting: "Give me something real or I am leaving. Give me Jesus or I am going to blow up!"

"I remember looking down at the pastors sitting on the platform. One of them was just shining. He had a brilliance about him that was hard to miss. He was so immersed in the worship and praise. So glad to be there. I knew I didn't have what he had. But I wanted it.

"I kept coming to church, always sitting in the balcony. Finally, on New Year's Eve, I asked Jesus Christ to take control of my life. After that I started attending prayer band meetings, an intercessory ministry of the church. It was in that atmosphere of prayer that God really began to penetrate my heart. As people prayed I would just sit and cry. I was deeply moved by the presence of God. Gradually, tenderly, God peeled away all the layers that had covered my hurt and pain and all my questions about life. As he did, I began to get better. I sensed so much love in that room that I was content to sit there and pray all day, for the rest of my life.

"But I had no desire to sing again. Music had left such a sour taste in my mouth. Of course nobody in the church had any idea about my career. They didn't even know I could sing. One weekend I attended a retreat for the prayer band. When it came time for the talent segment, I surprised myself by volunteering to sing a song called 'Hunger for Holiness.'

"As I sang, something happened inside me. The words weren't just the words of the song I happened to be singing but convictions that came from deep inside. I wasn't performing anymore. Pretty soon people began crying and praising God all over the place. I looked around and wondered what on earth was going on. Later, one of the pastors suggested I try out for the choir. I fought the idea a little because I still didn't want to sing. Finally I gave in because it seemed like God was asking me to. How could I say no when I knew it was his will?

"When you join the choir it's like joining an army because it's a place of discipline. God changes you and transforms you so that you can be a blessing to others. It's not a place for people who just like to sing or for people who always want their opinions to be heard. There are 275 people in the choir so how could we all keep expressing our opinions and get anything done? It's focused. It's intense and it's work. But it has been my place of blessing.

"Every song that Carol has given me to sing has affected me. She doesn't give solos just because she thinks you can sing them well. She gives you songs because she feels you will be able to express their message effectively.

"The song that affected the most profoundly is called 'You Were There.' It talks about how God was there when I was lost, how he rescued me and gave me hope. It goes on to say that it was God who dried my tears and delivered me from my fears and who promises he will never leave me. I had felt so alone when my father left and then when my musical career hit the wall. I wondered where God was. But he was there all the time. He hadn't forgotten me. When nobody else saw my tears, he did.

"When you are away from the Lord, a kind of darkness comes over you that makes it hard to see God. Your emotional confusion and your sin hides him. But that doesn't mean he isn't there. When you come into the light, you come into alignment with God and you begin to see how he's been working all the time. It's good to know that God was there—he was there through all my struggles and all my questions, and he'll always be there for me. I never shared my story with Carol, never auditioned for the song. She just gave it to me, and it was like singing my life story.

"After things started coming together for me, I met my future husband at the church, and we now have two beautiful children. That in itself is amazing because a few years ago I told the Lord: 'I don't want to get married. Please God, I am never having anybody's babies. No way!' You can talk to members of my family. They will tell you I am the last person they thought would ever get married and have kids. But my husband actually thinks I'm a good mother and a good wife! Now I am a suburban housewife. Urban, hip-hop, rapper, suburban housewife. Talk about both ends of the spectrum! And there's nothing I'd rather be doing than being at home with my kids and singing in the choir even though I've never worked so hard in my life."

God had seen the heartache of a young girl whose parent's marriage had suddenly crumbled. He knew about her attempts to make something of her life. He was there beside her as she ate alone in her apartment every night. When Pam finally got low enough to surrender her life to God, she began to realize that he had never left her. That he never would leave her.

So many of us wonder, like Pam did, why our lives seem to be stagnant or going nowhere. We may go through the motions of religion without having a real relationship with Jesus Christ. Just as God renewed Pam's sense of hope and blessed her with a new life, he will do the same for anyone who gets to the end of themselves and finally puts their trust in him.

Over the years, the choir has learned that a surrendered life is the key to experiencing God and being used by him to accomplish his purposes. When our lives match the lyrics, then we are truly singing.

LIVING THE LYRICS

Winters in New York can be brutal. Even so, I often see single mothers and their children in church during the worst kind of weather even though it's taken them more than an hour to get there by subway and bus. People who drive to church often have to park eight to ten blocks away, and taxis, vans, and charter buses bring groups of visitors from far away places. Sometimes on New Year's Eve people line up for hours, waiting outside in frigid temperatures just because they want to celebrate the New Year in the house of the Lord.

Is it the music, the preaching, or some clever program that draws them? Have we figured out a special formula that has made the church grow beyond all expectations? The answer, of course, is much simpler. People come because they are searching desperately for spiritual reality and love. For them, no obstacle is too great to prevent them from entering a place where they can hear God's truth and experience his love.

In many ways, the city is a hostile environment for Christians. Living here can make you really cling to God because, believe me, New York is not the Bible Belt, nor is the church part of the city's culture. Maybe that's why choir members take their ministry so seriously. We realize our job is not to perform but to lead people into the presence of God. In fact, the

Bible says nothing at all about one group of believers getting up on a stage to entertain another group of believers. King David didn't sing and dance before the Lord to entertain people but to worship God. No matter how hard you search, you can't find the idea of performance anywhere in the Bible.

It's true that we've had our share of opportunities to appear with well-known entertainers. We've been asked to perform at national political conventions, to appear in various motion pictures, and to back up top performing artists. But we haven't felt right about any of these invitations, because that's not what God has called us to do. Our ministry is to lead people to an encounter with Jesus Christ. For us, performance would be a giant step down.

In fact, the Bible says nothing at all about one group of believers getting up on a stage to entertain another group of believers. No matter how hard you search, you can't find the idea of performance anywhere in the Bible.

But we can't lead people to God unless we first allow him to fill us with his Holy Spirit and love. This is true not only for the choir but for everyone in ministry: for pastors, intercessors, Bible study leaders, and youth leaders. Unless your heart is full of God's love, you will never have the compassion you need to see people through his eyes. That's why when I audition a new choir member, I do more than listen to that person's voice. I try also to hear that person's heart because I would rather have lesser singers with sincere and loving hearts than great voices singing merely to perform.

Sometimes I hear people in churches talking about music as though the music itself were the answer. "That song really works," they say. But no song "works" when it comes to changing people's hearts. Only God can change our hearts. Just because a song provokes an emotional response doesn't mean it's working on a spiritual level.

WHO'S SINGING

I don't believe that God is looking for songs to anoint. Neither is he looking for perfect music. If he wanted perfection, he would simply command the angels to sing. No, what God is look-

> *Our ministry is to lead people to an encounter with Jesus Christ. For us, performance would be a giant step down.*

ing for are people available to be used by him to spread the gospel and see his name *alone* glorified.

That's how real ministry happens. Whether it's a sermon, a small group discussion, or feeding the hungry, the truth is the same. Those who really minister are those whose hearts have been emptied of self and filled with the grace and love of Jesus Christ.

I'll never forget an experience I had as a young girl in my father's church because it has shaped my understanding of the kind of worship that God is seeking. I can still picture the scene, forty years later. A woman stood up as we began to pray. She was a skinny white woman, not particularly attractive, not particularly gifted, at least when it came to singing. But when she opened her mouth and sang her praise to the Lord, hearts were drawn into his presence. Her love for the Lord was so evident that all you could see was the beauty of Christ in her.

Fortunately we've been blessed with some very talented people who really love the Lord, though sometimes it's taken a while to get their priorities in order. Brenda Davis is a woman who sang on the choir's first three albums. The day she joined, the soprano section increased in volume by thirty percent. Her voice was terrific. There was just one problem.

She had not yet learned the difference between performance and ministry.

Even though Brenda had sung professionally, I buried her in the back row. To choose a soloist, I need to hear more than a beautiful voice. Though God can use our voices, it's through our hearts that his love is communicated.

Remember, the choir is only as good as the hearts of the people who are in it, and God was still doing a work in Brenda's heart, shaping her personality in a way that would give him glory, rather than in a way that would bring her acclaim.

> *Remember, the choir is only as good as the hearts of the people who are in it.*

One day, Jim came home after performing a wedding ceremony for two ex drug addicts who had very little money. When Jim walked in the door that night, he didn't comment on the ceremony. Something else had caught his eye that day. Later he told me: "As I walked into the lobby, I saw someone on her hands and knees, carefully cleaning the legs of a serving table in order to spruce things up for the party after the wedding. I asked the head usher who it was that was helping with the little reception for these people. He said, 'Oh, that's Brenda Davis.'"

"'Brenda? How does she know these people?'

"'She really doesn't know them. She just knows they have little money and wants to help.'"

Over the last few months Jim and I had noticed Brenda at the altar, asking for prayer and then praying with others. When Jim saw her on her hands and knees that day, the first thing he said when he walked through the door was: "Carol, Brenda Davis is ready. It's time for her to sing."

So Brenda recorded solos on some of the choir's albums. Since then, she's gone on to become the editor of a magazine for Christian women, and she has also become a very dear friend. Whenever I think of the kind of person we want in the choir, I think of Brenda Davis, not because of her many talents but because of her servant's heart.

But how can you tell the condition of someone's heart? There's no sure way, of course, but a lot comes out by spending a little time talking with them. Anyone who makes it past the vocal part of the audition for the choir is interviewed either by me or by a member of my staff.

When I sit with eager applicants, I try to assure them that God has a plan for their lives. (We often have more than a hundred people audition for just ten to fifteen openings.) That's why I need to stay sensitive to his leading in the selection of new choir members. I ask them to tell me about themselves and their background. After a while I ask when they accepted Christ into their lives. Sometimes their answers make it clear that they really don't know him yet. I've sometimes prayed with people right at that moment and led them to the Lord.

During the course of the interviews I often meet people who have a deep faith in God. It's humbling to hear how God has worked in their lives. Their love for him is evident. These are the people I want to be a part of the ministry.

But there are others with outstanding voices who seem to have very little relationship with God. Talent alone is not enough. Some of the most talented people we audition may only be looking for a chance to sing in a big choir. For them, it's about status, not ministry.

During the interview I surprise people by asking a few personal questions. For instance, I ask who they're living with, because such a question often uncovers what their values really are. I remember one man who interviewed with Leroy, a member of my staff. When Leroy asked him who he lived with, he nearly bolted out of his chair. "What do you mean, who do I live with? That really isn't any of your business, Leroy. Look, I've sung in three different choirs, I've done solo work, and I've never been asked that question. I'm not answering."

The guy got up and left, and we never saw him again. Although I was sad to see him go, I believe it's not numbers that matter but who's singing. If an alto is on the note every single time but is living with a guy she's not married to, then she can't represent Jesus Christ and minister in our choir.

Of course I've made mistakes, sometimes inviting people in before they were ready. But I don't ignore the problems that surface. Instead, I tell people they have a choice. Either make things right with God or step down from the choir.

> *It's not numbers that matter but who's singing. If an alto is on the note every single time but is living with a guy she's not married to, then she can't represent Jesus Christ and minister in our choir.*

When someone passes the first interview they go on to see my husband. Jim usually talks to prospective choir members in groups of four or five, and I sometimes think he does his best to scare every last one of them away. "Look," he tells them. "You might be wondering why we've made such a production of your applying to join the choir. Let me explain why you've been voice tested, interviewed by Carol or one of her staff, and why you are now sitting in the office of the senior pastor.

"Carol and I have been working together for a long time and God has used the choir to bless the church in some unusual ways. In some churches the choir is just asked to sing a song or two before the sermon. In others, the choir sings and then leaves the building, not even staying for the service. God has done the opposite with us, using the choir in greater ways than just singing. I have often asked choir members to go out and pray for the congregation at large or to pray for those who need one-on-one ministry at the end of the service.

"Not long ago a woman wearing sunglasses came up to the altar for prayer. She was crying quietly as she stood praying, so I reached down and tapped her gently on the shoulder, asking if I could help. She took off her sunglasses and I saw an eye so swollen and black that it looked like she'd been hit by a prizefighter. Apparently, her husband, the man who was supposed to cherish and protect her, had beaten her up. She told me he had been selling and using crack cocaine, filling up the house with guns and drugs. His buddies were counting money and cutting drugs at the kitchen table, right in front of their two children. As soon as this woman confronted her husband, telling him to put a stop to it, he slammed his fist into her face.

"I knew she needed a pastor but they were all busy praying with other people. So I did what I've done a thousand times before and looked for an alto or a soprano whose attention I could get. Then I asked the choir member to pray with her and set up an appointment with a pastor. 'Call her every day for a week. Encourage her, give her the Word of God, be a prayer partner for her and then help her meet other members of the church.'

"That woman didn't need a song; she needed someone who could share God's Word and pray for her. I have to know that the people I'm sending to minister to others are serious about their faith. It doesn't matter at that point how well you can sing. If you join the choir, you'll be asked to do things that are only possible if you're very serious about spiritual ministry and sincerely walking with the Lord."

If Jim doesn't frighten them off, and if we both agree that a person would make a great addition to the choir, we invite them to join.

It's that simple—or complicated, depending on your point of view. But taking the time beforehand has saved us a lot of problems and has preserved the ministry of the choir over the years.

THE WORSHIP GOD SEEKS

Jesus said, "A time is coming and has now come when the true worshipers will worship the Father in spirit and truth, for they are the kind of worshipers the Father seeks. God is spirit, and his worshipers must worship in spirit and in truth" (John 4:23–24). So God is not just seeking any kind of worship but the kind that is given when you and I come before him in "spirit and truth." He is not looking for people who are play-acting or performing or who are merely praising him with their lips but not their lives.

I'm well aware that worship music has become a multi-million-dollar industry. And I know that technological advances have encouraged us to place more emphasis than ever on production. But as I travel around the country, I've seen too many worship leaders and teams performing worship music instead of leading the people into true spiritual worship. The danger I see is that those in the pews end up merely being spectators, following along mechanically but never engaging their own hearts in the kind of worship God seeks. The worship team may be singing beautifully, but their singing will have little impact if they haven't discerned where the people are spiritually in the whole process.

I urge churches never to value quantity over quality. It's important to avoid packing so many songs into a time of worship that it starts to feel like an endurance contest. As worship leaders, we do not need to fill up the time with music as if we are afraid of allowing a lull between the songs. Real worship also involves times of quiet waiting before the Lord.

I was visiting a church recently where the song leader jumped from chorus to chorus at a dizzying speed. The worship team was pumped. They were synchronized. Everything sounded great. But as I looked around, very few people seemed lost in worship. We must have sung twelve different choruses, but it was impossible to engage our hearts when we were trying so hard to learn song after song. It takes time for the words of a song to sink into our hearts. Sometimes it's better to sing fewer songs and sing them longer. Instead of feeling refreshed by God's presence at the end of our worship session, I felt like I had just completed an aerobic workout. I sat down exhausted.

I've seen too many worship leaders and teams performing worship music instead of leading the people into true spiritual worship. Those in the pews end up merely being spectators, following along mechanically but never engaging their own hearts in the kind of worship God seeks.

Millions of people today are hungry for an experience with the living God. They desperately want to encounter and praise him, not just see others performing. These people aren't looking for a show but something real. If we want to lead people in worship, we must begin by being vulnerable ourselves, worshiping God as we sing rather than putting on a show. If we come to God as a child would come to his father, asking the Holy Spirit to help us lead others into his presence through worship, the Holy Spirit will help us to be so taken up with God that others will be drawn to worship him too.

We must also take the necessary time. We can't merely rush through a pre-planned program of songs, but we must be sensitive to the leading of the Holy Spirit. He alone knows the spiritual state of the people and the exact need of the moment. Even simple *a cappella* singing from the heart means more to God than shallow but sophisticated musical productions.

Sadly, much of the so-called gospel music of today is shallow, with little connection to the biblical truths of our faith. Maybe these songs sound good, but much of the "crossover" variety contain lyrics that could just as easily be sung to a boyfriend or girlfriend. These songs may make an emotional impact but they don't leave a spiritual impression on our hearts. It's gospel music without the gospel.

> *Much of the "crossover" variety contain lyrics that could just as easily be sung to a boyfriend or girlfriend. These songs may make an emotional impact but they don't leave a spiritual impression on our hearts. It's gospel music without the gospel.*

I am painfully aware of the temptation to compromise when it comes to music. And it's no wonder. People feel strongly about the kind of music they like to hear. And if you lead a worship team or a choir, you can't escape the pressure. I wish I could say I've never compromised about something so important. But I have. A couple of years ago, people in the church were really pressing me to teach a song from a popular movie. It was a take off on an old hymn, but there was something about the song that just wasn't right, and I knew I shouldn't do it. I also knew people would think ill of me if I resisted. So I gave in and taught the song to the choir. Afterward, I got in my car and cried all the way home. By teaching the choir that song, I knew I had crossed a line I was never supposed to cross. If our worship is to be the kind God seeks, we have to be sensitive to his guidance as we select the music, no matter how strong the pressure is to go another way.

In addition to singing songs that have a certain depth, it's important to remember to lift up the name of Jesus as we sing. It's not unusual these days to be part of a worship service that goes for twenty minutes before Jesus' name is ever mentioned. But it isn't Moses or David who saved us and set us free and gave us a future full of hope. It's Jesus. Parts of the church seem to be drifting into an Old Testament ministry and emphasis, perhaps forgetting that it is the name *Jesus* that makes the demons tremble.

I haven't shared these details of how we approach worship in the Brooklyn Tabernacle to say there's only one way to lead worship or build a choir. But I do want to let you know how seriously we take it. I believe the principles we rely on for selecting choir members make sense for choosing people for any other ministry of the church. Yes, there has to be a basic talent—but talent isn't the most important thing. All the talent in the world won't accomplish anything of spiritual significance if it doesn't come from a heart that's truly yielded to God.

> *By teaching the choir that song, I knew I had crossed a line I was never supposed to cross. If our worship is to be the kind God seeks, we have to be sensitive to his guidance as we select the music, no matter how strong the pressure is to go another way.*

Morris Chapman has been a friend of Jim's and mine for years. He's a well-known songwriter and worship leader. You may have heard some of his songs, like "Bethlehem Morning," "Be Bold, Be Strong," or "Jesus, Your Name Is Power." Here's what he has said about music ministry:

"I believe we should be inspired by a choir but that each choir should be itself. I don't sound like anyone else. Carol's choir doesn't sound like anyone else. But if God has given you a gift then use it, respect it, allow God to give you the power to carry it out. The proof of God's blessing is not how good the choir sounds or how many records they've sold but how many lives have been changed because of them. I would encourage people not to imitate Carol's choir but to follow them as they follow Christ. Imitate their example of being faithful in prayer and dedicated to integrity and excellence. But don't try to do everything exactly as they do it."

Churches today rely more and more on experts to teach them how to do everything from developing a youth ministry to having effective outreach programs. While it's important to learn from others, the key thing to remember is that we can only be who God wants us to be. We must continually seek him in prayer, asking the Holy Spirit to develop and bless our ministry. When I teach workshops around the country, I try to discourage people from looking for a formula. Instead, I encourage choir directors and worship leaders to focus on the importance of having a surrendered heart.

OPEN TO THE SURPRISES OF THE SPIRIT

Even though we have a method for auditioning and interviewing people for the choir, I never want the method to take over. Instead, I want to remain open to the leading of the Holy Spirit. I'll never forget my first meeting with Marleen Healey and Josh Carroll. (Josh tells his story in chapter 3.) The two of them had come to New York from separate parts of the country to pursue acting careers. Both were brand new Christians—and you could tell. Their faces were shining the day I met them.

"We've only been Christians a few weeks," Josh told me during the interview. "We still live in the same apartment, but

I sleep on the couch and she sleeps in the bedroom." I found their honesty both refreshing and disarming. And though I seldom take new Christians into the choir, I couldn't help but feel God wanted them to be part of things.

I've never seen anyone who looks more like the all-American girl than Marleen. She's a beautiful young woman. I had no idea how different her life had really been until she told me the story one day.

"I grew up in Aurora, Colorado, a suburb of Denver. My mom always said I was the happiest kid around until I hit puberty. Unfortunately, depression runs in my family, and it really hit me hard. My emotions just went crazy. I was either really high or really low. My father is a doctor so he tried putting me on antidepressants, but it didn't work.

"In high school I gained a lot of weight and began to do poorly in class. Towards the end, I stopped going to classes altogether, except for theater and choir because those were the only things I cared about. Despite my love for acting, I never landed the roles I wanted because I was always a little too heavy. Finally, I decided I was going to do whatever it took to get the lead in the school play my senior year. That meant dropping twenty pounds, so I limited myself to one bagel sandwich a day. That was all I ate, and I exercised fanatically. After I lost the weight, I was suddenly popular. Guys especially liked me, and I was so insecure I would do just about anything to feel loved.

"Later, I used to bring my long-term boyfriend home with me and we would spend the night together in my room. My parents never objected. Anything to make me happy, I guess. But I wasn't happy.

"On my nineteenth birthday I announced to my parents that I was going to move to New York City to pursue an acting career. Really I just wanted to run away, and New York seemed like such an exciting place to live. Two weeks later, I climbed into my car and drove off, leaving my mother sobbing in the driveway.

"I felt so strong, so upbeat as I drove through Colorado, Kansas, and Missouri. But by the time I hit Pennsylvania I was an emotional wreck. What was I doing? I didn't know anybody in New York, didn't even have a job. But I kept driving.

"When I got to New York it was even worse than I thought it would be. I had an apartment, but I was afraid to leave it.

"Finally, two months after I moved to the city, I got up the nerve to go to an audition. A guy was standing in line behind me and we just started talking. His name was Josh Carroll, and we bonded instantly, probably because we were both so lonely and afraid. But even though we spent a lot of time together, we didn't get along. How could we? I was depressed and insecure, starving myself thin. And Josh was drinking all the time.

"Both of us had passed the audition and were hired as performers in a musical review that was staged at a resort in Wisconsin. I was thrilled to be acting anywhere but Josh was in the pits. To him this was the bottom of the totem pole. When we weren't working we just hung around. I chainsmoked while he drank.

"When Josh decided to break into the bar to steal beer, I didn't want any part of it. But I got arrested anyway. After spending a night in jail, I was handcuffed to another prisoner and then brought out into a common room. Josh was there in handcuffs too. What a sorry sight we were. We were released but warned to stick around to face a charge of burglary. Josh's dad drove all the way from Nebraska to take care of us. He was so patient with us, so loving. And he kept talking about God's desire to have a relationship with us. Because we were both so scared, we actually listened to him. And we prayed, asking God for a miracle, begging him to get us off. And he did.

"But our lives didn't get any better. As soon as we got back to New York we moved in together. Then our arguments really took off. Josh would get jealous, imagining I was looking at every guy who walked by. No matter how much I told him I loved him, he wouldn't believe me. And I would flip out, throwing dishes or anything else that came to hand. Before long everything we had was broken and there were holes in the walls. Josh kept drinking, and I became more and more depressed. Every time we slept together we began to feel guilty, knowing it wasn't right.

"We didn't have any friends to help ease the tension. At first everyone who met us loved us, thinking we were such a cute couple. But they would soon realize that Josh had a drinking problem and I had mood swings like crazy. Our constant arguing alienated everyone around us.

"Things got so bad that I couldn't even act anymore. Performing had always been a great escape for me because I could leave my depression behind by pretending I was someone else. But now even acting wasn't working for me.

"At one point, Josh signed an acting contract that took him out of town for three months. While he was away I worried I was going to lose him and started eating even less, working as a waitress in an all-night diner from 6:00 P.M. to 6:00 A.M. I was taking so many diet pills I couldn't think straight. I was angry all the time, and every night I threatened to quit. You can get away with that in a diner in New York because they have a hard time finding people.

"When Josh got back to New York we decided we needed to find a church. A customer at the diner handed me a pamphlet about the Brooklyn Tabernacle, and then one night Josh's uncle called, also suggesting we visit the Brooklyn

Tabernacle. Josh had told his parents we were looking for a church, and his mom had warned us that once we made the decision to go, the devil would do anything to stop us.

"That first Sunday, we barely made it. We were late and screaming all the way. I don't remember much about the service but the music, but the next day I felt so different. I can't tell you why. I felt happy, and it was strange to feel so good because I had been depressed for so many years.

"That night after church Josh started sleeping on the couch. But we still hadn't made a definite decision to give our lives to Christ. Then one evening at a prayer meeting, Pastor Cymbala began talking about a time in the Bible when God told the people there would be a 'famine of his word.' Then he got more personal, saying: 'God keeps speaking to your heart and if you ignore him, one day you aren't going to be able to hear him.' That night we were both hysterical. We didn't want God to stop reaching out to us. That was when we finally gave ourselves to Christ.

"Shortly after that we tried out for the choir. It wasn't that we wanted to be in the choir all that much. We just wanted somebody to know we were there. We wanted our questions answered and we wanted friends. We were so confused, so needy.

"Carol looked at us strangely as we talked to her during the interview, telling her about our situation. Then I saw tears coming down her cheeks. 'You know, there is nothing better than knowing Jesus,' she said. That was all I needed to hear. I knew then that there was hope. Things were going to get better.

"As soon as we got home after the audition there was a message waiting for us on the answering machine offering us a great acting job. It involved traveling around France and getting paid a thousand dollars a week for performing in a musical review. Immediately we pushed the erase button because we knew exactly who was behind that message. Someone was determined to keep us stuck in our old life, but we weren't going to take the bait.

"The church helped Josh find another place to live right away, and we made friends in the choir who helped answer our questions. I know that being in the choir is supposed to mean ministering to others. But I have been ministered to so much by being part of it. I no longer feel I have to earn anybody's love. Nor do I have to spend two hours in front of the mirror before I go out. I'm not afraid to leave my apartment, and now there's no more starving myself and no more depression. It has completely lifted.

"Even though God was doing great things in our lives, I wasn't sure what to think about my relationship with Josh. We still had a lot of resentment toward each other because of the awful things we'd said and done. Did God want us to stay together or break up? It would have been a whole lot easier to split up than stick it out and work through our difficulties.

"I remember looking over at Josh worshiping the Lord one day as we were singing in the choir. In that moment it was as though I heard God say: 'Stop focusing on the past and look at what I've done. Josh loves me and his life is in my hands. You don't have to worry that he's going to start

Carol looked at us strangely as we talked to her during the interview, telling her about our situation. Then I saw tears coming down her cheeks. "You know, there is nothing better than knowing Jesus," she said. That was all I needed to hear. I knew then that there was hope. Things were going to get better.

drinking again. I am going to take care of you both.' I knew then that God was giving us a new start.

"Among other things we had to learn boundaries because our boundaries had always been so extreme. For instance, we would only end an argument after dishes had been smashed and we were both hysterical. Some boundary! We both knew that without God our relationship would be impossible. But as we worked through these things, God gave us a genuine love for each other. We've also learned how to communicate and how to pray together. During the course of our stormy relationship, we'd seen terrible sides of each other. But these don't even exist anymore because of what God has done. Last year, on May 20, we were married, and I am so grateful to have Josh in my life."

Both Josh and Marleen are gifted people. But it wasn't their talent that impressed me the day they auditioned for the choir. It was the overwhelming sense of their love for Jesus. They both shone like new spiritual babies and their hearts were so pure and tender despite their recent past. Through a great deal of darkness, they had finally come to the end of themselves. There they met a God who had always loved them and who would stop at nothing to bring them to himself. They are the kind of people I am so proud to have in the choir.

Incredibly, God not only saved them but he saved their relationship as well, putting it on a whole new foundation. When I consider the way Marleen and Josh have changed, I am reminded of the words of the old song that says:

> Turn your eyes upon Jesus
> Look full in his wonderful face
> And the things of earth will go strangely dim
> In the light of his glory and grace.

THE SACRIFICE OF PRAISE

One of my favorite Bible verses reveals the nearness of God. It describes him not as a distant being but as a tender God who actually inhabits the praises of his people (Psalm 22:3). Since we know that God is everywhere at all times, this verse must be describing something much more intimate and personal. This has often been called the "manifest presence of God" in which God reveals some of his glory to the hearts of those who worship him. We experience his nearness, blessing, and help not when we are rehearsing again and again our doubts and complaints but when we are offering up our praises and thanksgiving. That is why this whole subject of worship and praise is so important to our churches and to our individual lives as well.

Whenever our praises go up to heaven, the Holy Spirit gives us fresh revelations of who God is, showing us how great his glory is. When I read the stories of people in the Bible who had dramatic encounters with God, I realize that many of them were overwhelmed by a revelation of God's glory.

When we see, as David did, that "the glory of the LORD is great" (Psalm 138:5), we also realize how small and needy we are by comparison. We are humbled in his presence just as Moses, Isaiah, and the apostle John were. We begin to realize that God is worthy not only of our praise but of the sacrifice

> *God's blessings are released and his victories are won not when we doubt him or complain about how tough we have it. Instead, God dwells with us to bless and help us as we live lives full of praise and thanksgiving.*

of our entire lives. We want to bow low before him for "he is great and greatly to be praised" (Psalm 96:4). When we experience the glory of God, the last thing we want to do is to put ourselves forward to seek the limelight. We can't give God glory while we are trying to get it for ourselves. In fact, God clearly says he will not "share his glory with another" (Isaiah 48:11). Any preacher, singer, choir, or church that wants to get the glory for themselves needs to have a fresh encounter with Jesus Christ. Our place is in the background so that God can be center stage all the time.

How easy it is for each of us to lose sight of this truth about God and his glory. It's easy to start compromising, to want to reserve a little glory for ourselves. After all, it's our talent the Lord is using. But this kind of attitude is spiritually dangerous because it grieves the Holy Spirit. When we catch ourselves seeking our own glory, it helps to remember that every one of us will one day appear before Christ's judgment seat to give an account of how and why we labored for him. It is there that our motives will be revealed, when Christ himself judges the quality of our work and gives us our eternal reward.

THE "ACCIDENTAL" BASS PLAYER

Joey Vasquez has been with the choir for twenty-seven years. He works on the church staff doing, as he says, "Whatever Carol doesn't want to do." The description doesn't entirely fit since I haven't yet convinced him to disguise himself as me so he can take on some of the public appearances I dread the most. But we're working on it. Joey joined us as a teenager, back when, in his words: "You only had to be able to walk and chew gum at the same time to get into the choir."

You might say that Joey was surprised into becoming our bass player. This is how he remembers it.

"I'd only been in the choir a couple of weeks and had made friends with the drummer, a guy named Sam. One day he invited me to his house before choir practice. When I got there Sam was fooling around with a bass guitar, trying to play along with a Christian album that he was listening to. I asked him if I could try it and then proceeded to stumble my way through a song. Shortly after that we headed to the church for choir practice. After our prayer time, Carol came up to me and said, 'Sam told me you know how to play the bass.'

"I was shocked. The guy must have been joking. I'd played the guitar a little before but never the bass. 'No, I have no idea how to play the bass, Carol.'

"'I think you're just being shy, Joey. Of course you know how to play the bass. Now help us out with the next song.'

"So right in front of everybody, with much fear and trepidation, I started playing the bass, and I've been playing it ever since.

"After being in the choir for about six years, we recorded our first album. But I wasn't on it. We used professional players recommended by the producer. That happened for the next few albums as well, which was fine with us because we knew our band wasn't yet ready for prime time.

"After about five or six studio albums, Carol decided that she wanted to do a live album with our own musicians because she wanted the choir to sound the same as they would if they were singing for one of the church services, something that the studio albums never achieved. Just before that time, I had taken a three-month leave from the choir for personal reasons and another brother from the church played during my absence. When I returned, I was excited to hear that we would finally be playing on one of the choir albums. To my disappointment, though, Carol informed me that she felt that the new bass player should play at least two songs on the album since he had been helping out during my absence. I did not think that this was fair because I had been playing faithfully for twelve years and he had only played for three months. Though I wanted to play on every song myself, I didn't say anything. After the album came out, we had the opportunity to minister at Radio City Music Hall for the first time. We were to debut our new album. Again, Carol said that she was planning to use the other bass player on a couple of songs. This time my disappointment just boiled over and a few days later I confronted her.

"'Carol,' I said, 'I've been playing for twelve years and I've never missed a choir practice. Why can't I be *the* bass player now that we're doing Radio City Music Hall?' Nobody uses two bass players during a concert.

"'You know what, Joey,' she said. 'I've thought about it, and it wouldn't be feasible to use two bass players so you are going to be the only one, but it shouldn't really matter who plays. The only thing that should matter is that God gets the glory.'

"That was all she said. All she needed to say. I suddenly felt very small. My ego had distorted everything. I hadn't been playing all those years so people would tell me how great I was. I'd been playing because I loved to worship God with the choir and loved to lead others in worship. So why should I let my ego take over now? Carol had delivered exactly the jolt I needed. From then on, I decided my goal in life would be to see that God got the glory no matter what.

"Not long ago a young bass player visited the church. He was only eighteen, but he could play circles around me. He was so good it was scary. But I didn't feel even a twinge of jealousy. I was just grateful for his talent; glad he was using it for the Lord. Before he left, he commented on how unusual it was for another bass player to be so encouraging to him. Most of the musicians he'd encountered had seemed threatened, as though he was out to take their jobs.

"I could never have been so free to enjoy that young guy's talent if Carol had not challenged me so much over the years. But she's been like an arrow pointing straight to God, not just with her words but with her life. If there is anything in me that won't glorify him, I know God will take it out. Sometimes the refining process is painful. God allows trials to shape us. But I don't dread it anymore. Because my goal isn't to avoid suffering but to give God glory with whatever circumstances I face.

"Something else Carol has done for me and the other musicians in the choir is to teach us to worship God with our instruments. Just because I'm playing an instrument rather than singing doesn't mean I can't enter into worship with everyone else. The great thing about Carol and the whole choir, really, is that none of us have forgotten who we are. We know God chooses the foolish things of this world. We believe he blesses us when we try to give him all the glory. May we never forget it."

> *Sometimes the refining process is painful. God allows trials to shape us. But I don't dread it anymore. Because my goal isn't to avoid suffering but to give God glory with whatever circumstances I face.*

Whatever ministry or work God has called you to, I hope you will see that what Joey talks about holds true for all of us. Whether you work in a church, a bank, a factory, or an all-night restaurant, the calling is the same—to bring glory to God wherever we are. We will begin to bear lasting fruit the moment we make this our primary goal.

ONE HUNDRED PERCENT

As I speak at various conferences around the country, I hear from a lot of choir directors who say they can usually count on about sixty percent of the choir showing up for rehearsal. People are busy, they say. Sixty percent is pretty good, they say. But I can hardly believe my ears. To tell you the truth, I can't understand it at all.

So when I talk to them I remind them that Jesus withheld nothing from us even to the point of dying on a cross. After Christ has given so much for us, how can we serve him with anything less than our all?

We expect a lot from people who join the Brooklyn Tabernacle Choir. We think it would be unfair to them and to the Lord if we didn't. So when people ask me what our attendance rates are I say close to a hundred percent. The only time anyone misses choir practice is when he or she is sick or faced with an emergency. Even then they notify their leader that they will be absent. They don't cancel because they've had a bad day or because they couldn't get to sleep the night before. They don't miss practice because they need to do their Christmas shopping or because they'd prefer having dinner with a friend. They want to be there. And if they don't, we soon find out and ask them to step down so someone else more devoted to the ministry can take their place. We feel this is the only way we can effectively approach the ministry God has called us to do.

Choir members are expected to be at two of the four Sunday services (3:00 P.M. and 6:00 P.M.), and we encourage them to attend the Tuesday night prayer meeting as well. Members know that pouting and moods are never tolerated because you can't lead others in worship when you're thinking about yourself and all your problems. Just think for a moment what would happen if only ten percent of the choir rolled their eyes at the same time because they didn't like something. That's fifty-four eyes at once! Of course we're human. Difficulties will confront each of us. But from the moment we're on the platform, we put our own personal concerns aside so that God can use us to minister to others.

Neither is the choir a place to insist on your opinions or to express your musical tastes. We don't vote on which songs we're going to sing on a Sunday. And we don't pay attention to whether someone is a "winter," "fall," "summer," or "spring" when choosing what the choir will wear. If you're in the choir, you're expected to sing the music with everything that's in you, even if it isn't your favorite musical style. Being in the choir is a privilege. In light of what other Christians face throughout the world what we ask of our choir members is hardly a sacrifice.

Jesus, of course, is the ultimate example of someone who worshiped God through the sacrifice of his life. His absolute surrender brought salvation and blessing to those who would believe. We as Christians are called to follow Christ's example of dying but not on a cross. We are called to die to our selfish plans and desires so that Christ can live in us. As we do this by God's grace we will inevitably discover the fulfillment and joy we are trying so hard to find.

DÁMARIS'S STORY

Jim and I have known Dámaris Carbaugh for nearly thirty years. Music is so much a part of her life that I wouldn't be a bit surprised to learn that she came into the world singing a song. When Jim and I invited her to sing at our little church on Atlantic Avenue, she was just a teenager. Since then she's recorded nine albums, developed an international ministry, and has become a featured soloist with the Brooklyn Tabernacle. Of all the songs she's recorded with us, the one closest to my heart is "He's Been Faithful." Though Dámaris never stopped going to church, she tells about a time in her life when she strayed far from God.

"Sometimes people look back on their lives and blame their unhappiness on their families. But I had nothing like that to drive me away from God, no violence, no drug or alcohol addiction, no terrible hurts hidden inside me. Instead, I had about the best childhood you could imagine. And though I never fell in with the wrong crowd or became a runaway, a dropout, or a drug addict, I did something that to me is far worse.

"I was born in the mid-fifties and spent a lot of time in church. My grandfather was the pastor of a church in the South Bronx, and my mother worked with him. Shortly after I was born, my parents moved to Cuba for a year and a half to do missionary work. Later, we spent a few summers in Bolivia and Peru, traveling from church to church as my mother preached and my father sang and played the piano. After that we spent several years in Puerto Rico. That was when I first fell in love with music. My father started a children's choir with only a few kids. I will never forget the day he taught the twelve of us to sing in two-part harmony. I couldn't believe how beautiful it sounded. I was so delighted that I looked around at the rest of the kids in the choir to see if they were as excited as I was. But no one else seemed to share my enthusiasm about this glorious new discovery.

"When I was eleven we moved back to New York, and I began to take voice lessons at Carnegie Hall from a little Italian woman. Though it was unusual to offer classical training to a child whose voice hadn't fully developed, this tiny woman must have decided I was ready when she looked up and realized I was already half a foot taller than she was—measuring five feet seven in my stocking feet. As for me, I loved those lessons. Nothing else mattered. Just music and singing.

"By the time I was fifteen I was involved in all kinds of performances, including high school productions of *Kiss Me Kate* and *The King and I*. If there was a talent show in New York, I was in it. After one such performance, a man in the audience approached me and said something my fifteen-year-old heart would never forget: 'I really think you can make it,' he assured me. 'You have what it takes to be a star.' That man told me what I had always wanted to hear. From then on I wanted to be famous.

"After that, he introduced me to a wealthy musician who became my producer. From there I began doing commercials in hopes that my earnings would fund a demo recording that would impress a major recording studio. I started singing jingles for companies like Coca Cola, Pepsi, Kentucky Fried Chicken, Minute Maid Orange Juice, and Wrigley's Double Mint Gum.

"When I was sixteen, I was also part of something called the Cortese trio, with my sisters, Debbie and JoAnne. We were a back-up group for my mother's traveling evangelistic ministry. I'm not sure how Pastor Cymbala found out about evangelist Aimee and her singing daughters, but one day he invited us to minister in the little church on Atlantic Avenue. I'll never forget walking into the sanctuary and hearing Carol playing the organ. I looked at my sister Debbie and whispered, 'Can you believe it?' The chords she played were gorgeous and so different from what you normally heard in church. From that point on, the music really grabbed my heart.

"Afterward I told my mother how much I liked the church. I surprised myself by saying it, because what was there to like? There were only about thirty people in the congregation and none of them were all that friendly. The church itself was located in an ugly little building where everything was falling apart. But I was drawn by something else, something deeper. Carol and Pastor Cymbala's hearts seemed so full of God. I remember thinking, 'I want to know God and I want to love him the way they do.'

"After that we came back to the church several times, singing during the services and then helping out at the Saturday night Teen Challenge events that Pastor Cymbala was hosting. It wasn't long until the Brooklyn Tabernacle became our church. I remember being part of the first Tuesday night prayer meetings that took place in the church basement. God's presence was so real and strong.

"All the while we were in church I was still pursuing my dreams of becoming a pop star. In 1980 I got married and my husband, Rod, and I moved to Charlotte, North Carolina, where he had a job with a Christian television station. By then I had worked with several different producers but still hadn't landed a recording contract. Then one day, without my knowledge, my producer submitted a demo to the American Song Festival. The grand prize for that year was a quarter million dollar recording contract with CBS records. My producer sounded excited when she called me early in 1983, toward the end of my first pregnancy. 'Dámaris, you made it. You're among the top ten finalists!'

"'Finalists for what?' I asked her. 'The largest pregnant woman in the United States?' I had grown so huge during my pregnancy that I'd been telling everyone I had my own zip code.

"But she wasn't kidding. She assured me I was in the running for a major recording contract. Shortly before I gave birth to my daughter, I got the news. Dámaris Carbaugh had finally made it. I wasn't yet performing at Madison Square Garden and I wasn't booked into London's Palladium, but I was about to release an album with CBS Records. My career, I thought, was about to take off.

"Still, I had never shared my dreams with Pastor Cymbala or Carol, perhaps because I knew it would grieve them to hear what I really had in mind. I thought they were maybe a little too fanatical. They didn't have the big broad mind I had, really the big sinful mind I had. I had forgotten the Scripture that says: 'Do nothing out of selfish ambition.' Well, I lived for one big selfish ambition. To lift up my name. To hear people say, 'There's nobody that sings like she does.' I had convinced myself there was nothing wrong with my dreams. The world makes big bucks. Okay, I would make big bucks. But of course I would be different from other famous people. After all, I was a Christian. I loved the Lord. And I loved my husband and my family and my church. I'd give a lot of money to missions, I reasoned. What could be wrong with that?

"In 1984 the album was released. It must have sold ten copies—six to my mother and four to me. But I kept trying. Kept going to new producers. Spent my own money to cut demos that were going to make me rich and famous.

"Then in 1988 Pastor Cymbala invited me on a trip to Argentina to minister to a small conference of pastors. One day we sang at a local church that was packed with people. I can't begin to tell you how long those people stood and listened and worshiped and loved the Lord. I was so impressed by their simple devotion that I knew something was missing in my own life. Suddenly I recalled the Scripture Jesus quoted to the Pharisees and knew he was speaking to me:

'These people honor me with their lips, but their hearts are far from me.'

"For sixteen years I had been pursuing a way of life that God had not chosen for me. I had spent so much time. So much money. So much energy. I had said over and over that I loved the Lord when really I loved pursuing my own dreams for my life. I wish I could tell you that a great godly sorrow came over me in that moment. But at first I only felt embarrassed and ashamed to realize how deceitful my heart had been.

"As soon as I got back to the United States I told my husband that I was no longer going to pursue a secular career. I also told Pastor Cymbala that I wanted to use my voice only to sing for the Lord. Instead of criticizing me for the foolish desires I had pursued for so long and for failing to confide in him, he set up a little audition and arranged for a major Christian recording label to come to the Brooklyn Tabernacle to hear me sing. Though the people were very gracious, the record company later wrote to me and the gist of their letter was this: 'Don't call us. We'll call you.'

"When I got that letter I felt so frustrated and upset. I didn't understand what was happening—or not happening. After all, I had made the big sacrifice. Given up my career dreams, acknowledged that my talents belonged to God. Why wasn't he putting them to good use?

"Then I began to realize that God was still trying to get through to me. It seemed as though he were saying, 'Dámaris, you think you've changed just because you've started singing different lyrics. But I know you, and I know your motives. You still want to hold onto that mike. I want you to come to the place where whether you sing or you don't sing, it doesn't really matter. I want you to be able to say that I am enough for you no matter what.' It didn't matter to God that I was now singing 'Amazing Grace' instead of

'Oh, baby, why did you leave me.' He was looking for a much deeper change in me.

"But I couldn't honestly say that God was enough for me. So I told him the truth and begged him for help. 'No, you're not enough, Lord. I can't muster it up. I can't lie to you. But you have to be enough, so you've got to take my sick heart and change it.' And that has been my constant prayer.

"I wish I could tell you that I no longer have an ego. It wouldn't be true. I know that I have to go to God every day, asking for his grace. That's why Jesus said: 'If anyone would come after me, he must first deny himself and take up his cross and follow me.' My ego has to be nailed to the cross on a daily basis. But now, I have so much joy as I yield to the Spirit. Truthfully, I have more joy singing at some small church where there are only sixty or seventy people than I would singing pop songs at Madison Square Garden. But I could not have said that several years ago. Nothing can explain the change that's happened inside of me but God and his grace.

"I recall that day back in 1984 when I headed into CBS headquarters just before the release of my big record. The recording company had assembled a group of key disc jockeys just to meet me, Dámaris Carbaugh, soon to be a star. I felt such a rush and a thrill that day, thinking my career was about to take off. But now, as I remember it, I feel no thrill whatsoever. Instead I can feel a cold chill creeping down my

But I couldn't honestly say that God was enough for me. So I told him the truth and begged him for help. "No, you're not enough, Lord. I can't muster it up. I can't lie to you. But you have to be enough, so you've got to take my sick heart and change it."

spine. Because it reminds me of how far away from God I was. The rush I felt at the thought of becoming rich and famous shames me more than if I had been a drug addict exulting over a fresh supply of drugs. Most alcoholics and drug addicts I knew had developed their problem because of trying to cover up some kind of deep pain. But I had no pain. No early traumas. No excuses. My childhood couldn't have been any better. No, what I was suffering from was the same thing that got Satan kicked out of heaven. I wanted the glory that belonged only to God. I was puffed up and full of pride.

"It wasn't as though I simply needed to make a career shift, changing, say, from interior decorating to architecture because for some reason that would be more pleasing to God. I had been pursuing my own plan for my life, not caring whether God wanted it for me or not. I began to see how horrible it was to pursue a life apart from God's intentions for me. When I finally did give up my dreams of becoming rich and famous, I thought I had made the ultimate sacrifice. I was upset when that Christian record contract didn't come through. But God had mercy on me even when I talked such nonsense and made a big deal out of my little sacrifices. Because, honestly, what has any of us ever really sacrificed? What have we left behind? Jesus Christ left his throne, left his glory. He left everything in order to die on a cross to save us. We left nothing.

The rush I felt at the thought of becoming rich and famous shames me more than if I had been a drug addict exulting over a fresh supply of drugs.

"I'm so thankful for God's patience with me. So grateful for how he has used Pastor Cymbala and Carol in my life. The truth is they have always made God wonderful for me. If two people can make you jealous for God, they're doing something right. And that's what I want—more of God and less of me."

Dámaris is a dear friend who has truly surrendered her life to Jesus. God is using her in incredible ways because she has said yes to him. May her story serve as a reminder of how God's plans far exceed our own.

THE SONG OF THE REDEEMED

New York is either the greatest place on earth or the craziest, depending on your point of view. I fell in love with the city as a child even though other members of my family never adjusted quite like I did. It seems to me now that God tucked a love for the city into my heart because he knew I would need it later on.

Regardless of whether you love it or hate it, you have to admit that this city is never boring. Walking down the street I can see every color of person God ever made. I can smell Thai food, soul food, fine French cuisine, and everything in between. The flavors of the city are as varied as the people who call it their home.

Because our city is home to people from every part of the world, it's impossible to have a church limited to only one ethnic group, that is, if you're serious about doing God's work in his way. New Yorkers are good at spotting phonies. They know if a church is being hypocritical by preaching that God is love without opening its doors to everyone in the neighborhood.

The church was never meant to be a place for some and not for others. Ministering in a city like ours offers a unique opportunity to show the world what God intends for the church. His love revealed in so many different kinds of people offers a powerful contrast to the constant racial tension we see around us. Unlike the rough and abrasive attitude that prevails in the city, people in our church have found a way to love each other regardless of their color or cultural background.

I know this is true because I see it every day and because I am a white woman in an ethnically diverse church who is loved regardless of the color of my skin. The truth is that race has never been an issue in our church. By God's grace, we won't allow it to become one. Although I'm Caucasian, my cultural experiences have consisted of a mixture of influences from various nations around the world including Middle America.

WORLDS BEYOND MY OWN

By the time I was five years old, I already knew there were worlds beyond my own. The year before moving our family to Brooklyn, my father resigned his pastorate in Chicago and became an itinerant preacher. While my older brother and sister spent the year living with my grandmother in Kansas and going to school, I was happily sandwiched between my parents in the front seat of our car, watching America pass by outside our windshield. Most of the churches we visited that year were small, full of people who knew how to make you feel at home. Though we never stayed long in one place, we felt like we were part of an extended family that loved God and wasn't afraid to show it. I remember camping out once in a field in Arkansas during an all-day sing, featuring various gospel groups. Everybody just sat around their tents and enjoyed sharing the warm summer day together. I remember, too, all the little choirs that were woven into the fabric of the churches we visited.

My father, a man who has so greatly influenced my view of the world, was never the least bit small in his thinking. Not the least bit narrow or sectarian. His view of God's kingdom was too big to confine it to one expression of the church. He loved the world and showed it by the life he lived, traveling across America to preach the gospel and later throwing open the doors of his own church to every color of person and then making countless missionary trips overseas. During the last several years of his life he spent most of his time traveling, making more than 200 overseas trips to places around the globe. Sometimes he would bring home tapes of congregational worship from the countries he had visited. We heard music from Ghana and Kenya as well as the wonderful music of Brazil. The intensity and uniqueness of those simple songs left an indelible impression on my musical ear and on my heart. Neither could I help but be influenced by the variety of musical styles I was exposed to in New York.

So it never occurred to me that God's house should be anything exclusive. I expected it to be filled with every kind of person imaginable. It wasn't just a philosophy that my father imparted to me but a practical reality that surrounded me every day. That's why it is so hard to categorize the choir. We're not black gospel. We're not a traditional choir. We have our own sound; a blending that has come from many different cultures. Our friend Morris Chapman says it this way: "The choir has such a tremendous cultural blend that you can't pick out a black sound or a white sound. It's a cross-cultural sound that is hard to define."

A TASTE OF HEAVEN

David Ruffin, whose story is told in my husband's book *Fresh Wind, Fresh Fire,* tells how the music seemed like a "taste of heaven" to him one Easter Sunday a decade ago.

"I was a drunk, living in an abandoned truck. I'd been homeless for a number of years, lucky, I guess, to be alive. One morning, as I was sitting on the stoop at the back of the church finishing off a bottle of wine, I heard a sound like nothing I'd ever heard before. It came from inside. I could hear the singing and the clapping, and though I can't remember the name of the song it seemed like a calling from God. It was like he was telling me this might be the last chance I would ever get to come into his house. Even though I was afraid people would reject me because I was such a filthy mess, I went inside. That's when I heard a woman telling how God had solved her problem with drugs. Everything she said was exactly what I needed to hear. I needed the Jesus she was talking about. Without him, I knew I would die on the streets.

"The music I heard that Easter Sunday in 1991 helped save my life. After that, God got hold of me and brought me to himself and cleaned me up. Now I have a wife and kids and a good job at the church.

"One of the songs that has affected me the most is one that Carol and Oliver Wells wrote together. It's called 'Holy Like You.' The words express so much about what I want my life to be. I used to think that the only thing I wanted was another drink or more drugs. Now I only want to be like Jesus."

Music, as David Ruffin experienced, can be used to draw us toward something in a powerful way. That's why it is such a unique tool for either good or evil, depending on its source. Often the words and music of a song can open a person's heart so that they become more receptive to the Word of God or to hearing how God has worked in another person's life. I've heard ministers say that it's so much easier to preach a sermon after music has prepared the hearts of the people who are about to hear it.

When the choir sings, the Holy Spirit sometimes moves upon people in ways they don't understand. Suddenly they begin to feel peace or joy, despite the fact that their lives are anything but easy. People who don't know the Lord may not realize what's happening to them. They have to hear the message of the gospel to understand. That's why we no longer do concerts unless Jim or someone else preaches or someone shares the story about how their life has been changed by the power of God. It would be like working hard to prepare the soil in a garden and then forgetting to plant the seed into the ground afterward.

One of the songs the choir has sung over the years is called "Favorite Song of All." I think the chorus of this beautiful song expresses the reason why people in our church love each other despite their racial and cultural differences:

> *Music, as David Ruffin experienced, can be disarming, slipping past our defenses to pierce our hearts in surprising ways. That's why it can be such a powerful agent for either good or evil, depending on its source.*

> But His favorite song of all
> Is the song of the redeemed.
> When lost sinners now made clean
> Lift their voices loud and strong,
> When those purchased by His blood
> Lift to Him a song of love,
> Nothing more He'd rather hear
> Nor so pleasing to His ear
> As His favorite song of all.

Each of us in the choir and in the church belongs to God because of what Christ has done in our lives. Why else would we be here? In fact, we would never even know one another if it wasn't for Jesus.

In addition to all the different cultures and customs that come together in the church, we have people who have lived in very different circumstances from our own. Sometimes their stories have been so heartbreaking that Jim and I can only marvel at the way God has worked to restore their lives.

"SOMEONE TO HOLD ME"

Many Americans feel pressured and anxious about their lives. Sometimes we think we have it pretty rough. But most of us haven't a clue how fortunate we are. Until, that is, we hear the story of what other people have suffered. Then we realize that millions of people would change places with us in a second if only they had the chance.

About three years after we were married, Jim and I accepted an invitation for Thanksgiving dinner from one of the members of our church in Newark. Jean Freeman was a single mother, rearing five little ones by herself. She was part of the first small choir I had so nervously invited to practice a song in my home. I didn't know it then, but Jean would one day become like family to us. She and her children lived in a housing project for low-income people, many of whom were on public assistance as she was.

We couldn't help but notice how clean her sparsely furnished apartment was. Even more noticeable was the atmosphere. We felt a sense of peace and love as soon as we walked through the door. All Jean's children were neatly dressed as we sat down together to enjoy the meal she had so generously prepared. At that time, I knew little about her. What I learned later would amaze me. A small, soft-spoken woman, Jean looks like she's in her mid-to late forties rather than her early sixties, surprising given the kind of life she has lived.

"As far back as I can remember, I just wanted to be held. I knew my mother loved me but she never said much and I only saw my father once. He came to the house when I was a little kid. I remember looking at him through the window but don't remember a thing about his face. He never touched me. Never held me. Never called me on the phone or sent me a birthday card. He died when I was eight.

"When I was only five, my mother got a live-in job, but she couldn't bring my older sister and me with her. So we just moved from house to house—staying with whoever would board us for a while.

"The best home I ever had was with my grandmother, who loved us and took good care of us. I remember her giving me a bath and scrubbing my back. It felt so good to have someone touching me that I wanted to sit in that bathtub forever. I never knew why she couldn't keep us.

"Finally we ended up in foster care, and my sister and I lived in about every street in Asbury Park, New Jersey. Six months here, a year there. We had no foundation. Nobody to hug us and tell us what great kids we were. Nobody to keep us clean or make us do our homework. We had to learn everything ourselves. So as soon as I figured out how to write, I signed my own report cards, forging my mother's signature.

"When I was thirteen my mother married again, and my sister and I moved in with her and her new husband. It seemed like a new chance for us. But it became a nightmare because my stepfather was an alcoholic who never did a lick of work. I remember going to school hungry most mornings. At least in foster homes we had enough to eat. Now the only sure meal of the day was lunch, when we'd get cream cheese and jelly sandwiches at school. It didn't make things any easier to come home from school and see my stepfather sitting at the kitchen table cramming his mouth with food. Though I'd been receiving a monthly social security check since my father died, I never saw a penny of it. Didn't matter whether I needed new shoes or my clothes were wearing out. The money had to go for food. With my mother, my stepfather, their three children, my sister, and I to feed, there was never enough to go around.

"My fourteenth year was one to remember for all the wrong reasons. One day, I came home from school and found that everything we had was packed up.

"'Where are we going?' I asked.

"'I don't know,' was all I could get out of my mother.

"My stepfather hadn't paid the rent, so we'd been evicted. I remember all our stuff being packed into a little truck. I sat so still and scared, wondering what was going to happen next. It was March but my heart felt colder than the air outside.

"By then I had finally made it into the eighth grade. I wasn't proud to be fourteen and still in the eighth grade, but at least I was looking forward to graduating in May, especially since the girls always got to wear pretty white dresses. But now there would be no graduation for me because we were leaving the district.

"After a while my stepfather moved us to New York. But things weren't any better there. When I came home from school I was the one who washed all the diapers and helped keep the three little kids clean and took them for a walk to get a little fresh air. It wasn't long before my mother became pregnant again—this time with twins.

"Just before they were born, I visited one of my aunts for the summer. When I decided I couldn't stand the thought of returning home, she found me a live-in job. Even though I only made seven dollars a week, I was at least living with people who were kind to me. And for the first time in a long time I had enough to eat.

"By the time I was in my early twenties I noticed that everybody was getting married but me. I was so lonely that I made the mistake of falling for the first guy who showed any interest. I had no idea what that mistake would cost me over the next several years. Though my husband didn't drink that much or take drugs, he seemed to enjoy beating me just to make himself feel big. We had four children together, and every time I went to the hospital to have another baby, I went with bruises on my body. But I was just too scared to do anything about it.

"At one point we lived in a housing project where he was carrying on an affair with another woman who lived there. I didn't know what was going on at the time but later realized that he had stopped paying the rent to get rid of me and the kids.

"After we were evicted, the kids and I moved into an apartment that was full of rats—it was all I could afford. I'll never forget walking through the living room toward the kitchen when one of the rats started coming at me. At first I thought he was trying to play with me. I'd never been around rats before and didn't realize I was being attacked. It was so bad that I used to sleep with my shoes on the bed so I could throw them at the rats whenever they would try to climb up. Once I lined the kids up on the couch while I ran and did the laundry: 'Don't move. Keep your feet up. Don't get down,' I warned them. The older ones watched the younger ones, and I prayed the rats would leave them alone.

"Finally, some relatives got us out of that place and we moved to East Orange, New Jersey. That's where I made another mistake. I got involved with a married man, and soon I was pregnant with my fifth child.

"Though I didn't know a lot about God, I knew my grandmother had believed in him and that she had prayed for my sister and me. We had also lived in a pastor's home once when we were in foster care. I remember the lady pastor praying with us at the front of the church. I know now that I experienced God as she prayed. But it felt so strange at the time that I ran to the back of the church and just stood there, unable to respond.

"One day a woman from the Newark Gospel Tabernacle came knocking on the door, talking about Jesus. I figured it would be good for the kids to go to church so I began sending them. But I wouldn't go myself.

"She came back a few days later asking for me. 'Jean, are you there? Come talk to me,' she called up the stairs. She was a big woman, and I figured she was too fat to make it up three flights of stairs to my apartment, so I pretended not to hear her. But she came huffing and puffing anyway, and as soon as she walked through the door of my apartment she got right to the point.

"'Jean, you coming to church?'

"'No, I don't feel good.'

"'You've got to stop playing around and get right with the Lord,' she told me.

"I don't know why but I started crying. God seemed to be reaching out for me.

"So I began attending the church, and pretty soon my boyfriend noticed a change. 'You better stop going to that church. Somebody is messing with your head,' he warned me, like I was in some kind of mortal danger.

"Right then I knew I needed to stop seeing him. What we were doing was wrong. After that he tried to talk me into getting back together, but I told him I had found my true love and it was Jesus.

"So I kept going to church, and that's where I met Carol and Pastor Cymbala. I was part of Carol's first choir. Right away I thought they were the nicest people. And Pastor Hutchins, Carol's father, he was the most loving person I ever met. If I could have chosen a father for myself, it would have been him.

"The Lord drew me so strongly to himself that I just stayed in prayer all the time. He became such a friend to me, taking away my fear and giving me peace. One of my favorite songs has been sung at Billy Graham Crusades: 'His Eye Is On the Sparrow'—because that's how God is for me. Whenever I hear that song, I realize I don't need to be upset because he is with me, loving me and protecting me.

"Gradually my life began to straighten out. I even got my high school diploma when I was in my late thirties. When the Cymbalas moved to the church in Brooklyn I went with them.

"Even though I know the Lord, I've had some hard times. I lost one of my sons on the street one day, shortly after we moved to Brooklyn. He was shot outside a movie theater. Pastor Cymbala had to call me out of choir one Sunday to tell me Eric was dead. When you lose a child like that, it's so hard. Where can you find comfort? How can you find peace? But I believe God knew all about Eric, about his weakness, about everything he'd been going through. Shortly before his death I remember seeing him sitting on the floor of his room listening to one of the choir tapes over and over again. The songs were about salvation, about God's love. I believe God got a grip on him then, despite his troubles.

"Another one of my sons left home ten years ago, and I haven't seen him since. I pray he's alive and that God will somehow get through to him.

"A lot of people might look at my life and say, 'How can you possibly believe in God after everything you've been through?' But God has been the best friend I've ever had. He loved me when nobody else would. He's come and straightened me out emotionally. He's helped me care about people, even the ones who bother me the most. Now I pray for them instead of criticizing them.

"And I'm so glad to be in the choir. Because when we sing, it's not just words. We're not going to get up and sing some song to make you feel good. Through the choir, I've learned not to be so lonely. Because my eyes are not on myself or on my problems but on how I can love God and serve others.

> *A lot of people might look at my life and say, "How can you possibly believe in God after everything you've been through?" But God has been the best friend I've ever had.*

"Not long ago I bumped into two thugs on the bus. One of them was hanging onto a strap, leaning right over me. He had no teeth and his breath was foul. Even though I'm a little woman, I wasn't the least bit scared of those two guys. Instead I started telling them about the Lord. When I got off the bus I wondered what had come over me. Where did I get that boldness? I know God is still working in me, making me more interested in other people than I am in myself. Now I can love people I used to be afraid of. When God does that kind of thing, you can't help but believe in him, you can't help but know he's real."

Jean has lived a life that's been filled with one heartbreaking loss after another. I find it hard to imagine the loneliness of a childhood like hers or the brutality she suffered in her marriage. She's had even more heartbreak than she's told you about in these pages. But Jean isn't complaining. She's not feeling sorry for herself, and she's not letting the hard things in her life stop her from believing in Jesus. She knows too much about him to do that. Instead, she's singing the song of the redeemed along with David Ruffin, and Josh and Marleen Carroll, and Pam Pettway, and me, and so many others who know the love and power of Jesus. It's not the color of our skin that unites us, nor the similarity of our backgrounds but the shared experience of having a Savior who loves us. That's what keeps us going, that's what knits us together and makes us who we are—the body of Christ.

THE MOST EXCELLENT WAY

Six years ago my father suffered a major heart attack. As soon as we heard the news, Jim and I raced to Florida, hoping to arrive before his condition worsened. When we entered the room, I saw a man whose life was ebbing away. Dad was hooked up to various machines with tubes protruding everywhere. He didn't greet us with a friendly embrace, nor did he notice the tears that were being shed on his behalf as the family gathered around his bed. He was unconscious all the time we were there. Jim and I spent the week, watching and waiting with him until the day he died. In between the tears, we had such a strong sense of my father's love, as though he were preaching to us from his hospital bed.

It was a sermon without words. There were none needed. His life spoke it all. As Jim and I and other members of our family stood by his bedside remembering his life, what we recalled about Dad didn't center on the many sermons he had preached or the churches he had served or the mission trips he had made. What we remembered most was his love. It is what we remember still.

If at the end of your life those who knew you were to define you by one thing, what would it be? What is the impression you are leaving on the world? If you are seeking to follow after God and to reflect him in everything you do, the outstanding quality in your life should be love. The Bible tells us that God is love. It's incredible that such an awesome God would allow himself to be defined by just one word, but apparently that word is enough. Yet is this the emphasis of our Christian walk today? Are we satisfied to pursue this virtue above all others? There is one great command in the Bible. It is not a command to have a big church, a great choir, or a successful preaching ministry. God commands us to love.

Since showing love is not always glamorous and may not bring us recognition, its value often goes unappreciated. Yet if love is not the source of everything we do, the results will not please God. In First Corinthians, Paul says, "And now I will show you the most excellent way! If I speak in the tongues of men and of angels, but have not love I am only a resounding gong or a clanging cymbal. If I have the gift of prophecy and can fathom all mysteries and all knowledge, and if I have a faith that can move mountains but have not love, I am nothing. If I give all I possess to the poor and surrender my body to the flames, but have not love, I gain nothing." Truly, as Paul tells us, love is the most excellent way. It is the great standard by which God will evaluate our lives at the judgment seat of Christ. Though our selfish efforts might bring us the praise we desire on earth, God knows our hearts and without his love we have surely "gained nothing."

I know from personal experience that love is not the road our flesh naturally wants to take. Love takes humility and patience. It often involves sacrificing what we want for the sake of someone else. It sometimes leaves us vulnerable so that other people take advantage of us. Still, Jesus repeatedly told us to love one another. It was by this that men and women would know we were his disciples. The church is to display a love that causes the world to marvel. Is this evident among us today? In the midst of our denominational squabbles, racial divisions, and endless church splits, is Christ truly being reflected by his people?

Imagine that someone gave you a valuable antique. Suppose you had never seen anything so beautiful, so skillfully made, so delicate. Because you recognize its value, you handle it gently, cherishing it with all your heart. You would undoubtedly do all you could to protect it from harm.

If we as believers would make such efforts towards caring for something of mere monetary value, then how much more should we strive to guard over the body of Christ? After all, we are the church of God, which has been purchased by the blood of the Savior (Acts 20:28).

The world places its values on abilities, possessions, and accomplishments. God, however, honors what's done out of love, no matter how big or how small. But how do we as believers live out the kind of love God has called us to? It's a love that we cannot manufacture no matter how we try. True love can only be born of the Spirit of God.

WHEN THE SPIRIT IS GRIEVED

Whenever I am approached by choir directors looking for some kind of method to help their choirs minister to people's hearts, my answer is always the same. You can build the best choir in the world, but unless the Holy Spirit anoints it, your singing will never have a spiritual impact on people.

That's why week after week I remind the choir how important it is for us to yield to the Holy Spirit. Unless the Spirit has control of our lives and ministry, we will end up merely going through the motions without allowing God to change anyone's heart as we sing. It's so important to remember that Scripture says: it is "'not by might nor by power, but by my Spirit,' says the LORD" (Zechariah 4:6).

But the Holy Spirit, who is likened in the Bible to a dove, is very gentle in his dealing with us. This is why the Bible warns us to not grieve the Spirit of God (Ephesians 4:30). One of the things that breaks God's heart is disunity among his people. His Spirit is quenched whenever the church is infected with sins of gossip, fighting, and divisive attitudes. Scripture poses a question we should make a habit of asking ourselves: "How can two walk together unless they be agreed?" (Amos 3:3). Too often choirs and other ministries of the church miss out on what God has for them because of internal divisions that are never dealt with.

Whenever I am approached by choir directors looking for some kind of method to help their choirs minister to people's hearts, my answer is always the same. You can build the best choir in the world, but unless the Holy Spirit anoints it, your singing will never have a spiritual impact on people.

I remember my father coming home after a church board meeting one day when I was a young girl. This time, he didn't step lightly through the door with his characteristic smile. Instead, he seemed worn and beaten down. The board had been at it again, fighting over minor issues. My father, who had the gentlest of hearts, simply could not take the continuous bickering and division. Because of it, he eventually left his position at that church.

Because of what he suffered, Jim and I have always carefully protected the unity of the church by the grace of God. We pray for it and strive to impress members of the church that we won't be able to serve God as he wants us to unless we have unity. We mention it everywhere we can—in staff meetings, during interviews for positions at the church, at Sunday services and

Tuesday night prayer meetings, and whenever the different ministries of the church meet together. Because God's grace has so far preserved our unity, we have been able to experience the truth of the Scripture that says: "How good and pleasant it is when brothers live together in unity" (Psalm 133:1). We know that God is greatly pleased when his people are united in heart and spirit.

Years ago I wrote a chorus that expresses a prayer for this unity among all believers:

> Make us one Lord
> Make us one
> Holy Spirit, make us one
> Let your love flow
> So the world will know
> We are one in You

When you tune in the nightly news, it doesn't take long to realize how little unity there is in this world. It seems that arguing and fighting and backbiting are common, everyday experiences. If these things also go on in the church, why would anyone want to join us? Why would they believe what we say about God's love and his power if we can't even love one another?

When Jim interviews applicants for the choir, he always stresses the importance of unity:

"Look," he tells them, "a choir is never any better than the members who belong to it. You have been blessed with the talent to sing. But that's not the crucial thing when it comes to belonging to the choir. What's important is the state of your heart, because the Holy Spirit only fills people who are serious about following God. And the choir can only be effective if the Holy Spirit anoints it.

"What a tragic waste of time and energy it would be if the blessing of God were grieved away by animosity or gossip despite all the hard work and prayer of the choir. Being part of the choir can provide you with an incredible opportunity to touch people's lives, but you can squander it if you don't understand how the Spirit works.

"So if you join the choir, we ask you never to talk negatively about another choir member when they are not present to explain or defend themselves. That kind of divisive behavior will force us to take immediate action, since the spirit of gossip and fighting is a disease that spreads through the whole body, quickly harming the work of the ministry. All of us, including myself, are frail people. We sometimes make mistakes that hurt and offend others. But the only biblical way to handle these difficulties is to go to the one who has hurt you and then make it right with the help of God. We can never allow backbiting and slander because those sins affect the whole church.

"In order to do God's work effectively, we must do it with all our hearts and in a spirit of love."

Despite our best efforts, we still sometimes have problems. When I recognize a problem, I try to deal with it quickly, because I know that whatever I don't confront will eventually confront me. But by then the problems will be much bigger.

A few years ago, a woman was corrected by a choir leader for failing to follow rules clearly laid out in choir regulations. Instead of complying she took offense and began accusing her leader of picking on her because he was Puerto Rican and she was black! When we confirmed that she was saying this to other members of the choir, we asked her to step down for a season. She reacted by leaving the church, and though we were sad to see her go, we had to guard the treasure God had given us—"the unity of the Spirit through the bond of peace" (Ephesians 4:3).

STEVEN'S STORY

Perhaps the greatest sign of our unity as followers of Christ is the peace and love that exists between people of different racial backgrounds. Steven Wells, a surgeon who practices at a local university hospital, had been a Christian for a number of years before attending our church. When I invited him to join the choir, I had no idea that he had once been filled with hatred for people like myself. He seemed like a man who wanted to serve the Lord with all his heart.

> *Whatever we don't confront will eventually confront us. But by then the problems will be much bigger.*

Steven grew up as a black Muslim, practicing a form of Islam that mixes black nationalism with hatred of white people. Because of how God has worked, that poisonous hatred has vanished from his life, leaving no trace.

"My mother was born in the Virgin Islands, but my father's family came from North Carolina. Even though he was a few generations away from slavery, he knew how terribly his family had been treated, and he saw that black people were still sometimes treated harshly. That instilled in him a great hatred for whites. Becoming a black Muslim just fueled that hate. So I grew up as a black Muslim believing white people were evil and cruel. I also grew up hearing my father talking about how whites were always depicting Jesus with blond hair and blue eyes, trying to make him look white.

"Every night my dad would sit down with my brothers and me and teach us about God. He would talk about Allah and about the ways of Islam and about the submission required of a Muslim. We prayed in Arabic five times a day facing toward the city of Mecca as all Muslims do. We were a very religious family, and I believed it all until I was about fifteen years old.

"When I was in my teens I started playing basketball with a boy who was always talking about Jesus Christ. But the Jesus he talked about didn't match the one I read about in the Koran. The Jesus I knew was a prophet who paled in importance next to the prophet Muhammad. But the Jesus he spoke of, the Jesus of the Bible was a Savior who was also God. The more we talked and argued about our different versions of Jesus, the more confused I became.

"One of five kids in my family, I was always curious about everything. My brothers used to call me 'the brainy one' because I loved reading and always wanted to know how things worked. Now my logical mind had to find out the truth about Jesus. So I kept looking for facts and more facts. In addition to gathering facts, I started perceiving that Jesus actually worked in people's lives. That's when things changed for me. It wasn't just intellectual curiosity that was fueling my search. I really started to thirst for him. I got to the point where I not only wanted to find out the truth but I wanted to accept it, believe it, and live by it.

"The Jesus I came to know was human and close to me. He came to earth to seek me, to show me compassion, to show me God's love. That view of God was foreign to me because the Muslim god is far away. He has no real contact with you on a personal level. But I began to see that Jesus is the one who comes down and touches you, he talks to you, and he's precious to you. He feels what you're feeling and is touched by your infirmities. And that was what drew me and caught me and won my heart.

"Becoming a Christian revolutionized my life. It became clear to me that God had created the different races and that he wanted them to worship him together. Hatred of any kind, I began to see, was anti-God, and it would rob me of the true blessing of finding God. Because I was serious about embracing the God of the Bible, I decided I would have to learn to love everyone, including white people.

"That wasn't an easy thing for me to do at first because it went against everything I had ever learned about the differences between blacks and whites. But once I realized that the love I needed didn't come from me but from God and that it was shed abroad in my heart by the Holy Spirit it got a lot easier. I could do it through the grace of God.

"My faith in Jesus created a huge rift between my father and me. Things got so heated that one day he finally told me: 'Just leave my house. I can't have anyone worshiping the Jesus of the Bible in a Muslim home. It just won't work.' That was when my journey with God moved to a whole new level. Now I didn't just have to believe that Christianity was intellectually true, I had to trust Jesus for everything because I had no money and nowhere to live.

"Soon after my father threw me out, a Christian family took me in, and then one of the elders at the church I was attending gave me a furnished apartment and told me I didn't need to worry about the rent. The words of Psalm 27 became very real to me during that time: 'Though my father and mother forsake me, the Lord will receive me.' From then on the church was like a family to me.

"Without the support of my own family, I finished high school and went to college in the Bronx. Then I went on to medical school for four years all by the grace of God.

"I came to the Brooklyn Tabernacle after attending another church for several years. But I came in hurting because by then I was suffering the pain of a broken marriage. My feelings of loneliness and rejection and my need for God's love were what brought me into the balcony of the church. The music literally rose from the platform where the choir sings up to the balcony and into my heart, touching me and enabling me to freely praise God. It flowed over my mind and soul and caused broken pieces to come together in a way I can't even explain. Now as a member of the choir I feel so privileged to sing the music that touched me so powerfully in order to reach out to others.

The music literally rose from the platform where the choir sings up to the balcony and into my heart, touching me and enabling me to freely praise God. It flowed over my mind and soul and caused broken pieces to come together in a way I can't even explain.

"Eventually my father and I reconciled. I spoke to him again about Jesus a couple days before he died, and we talked about salvation. By then he was suffering from cancer in his lungs and brain. It seemed like there was a breakthrough that day. Every other time there was always a wall. But that day he said, 'You know what, I'm willing to consider a different Jesus.'

"We never got much further than that, but when he died my brother told me he found him on his knees. And it just caused me to wonder what it was that had brought him there. I guess I'll never know. But one thing I do know is that I told him all about the love of Jesus, and he saw the results in my life."

When Steven Wells received Christ into his life, he encountered a love so powerful that it overcame the prejudice he learned as a small child. God's grace has enabled him, not just to tolerate white people, but to love them as brothers and sisters in Christ and men and women created in God's image.

BEST FRIENDS

When you're living in the love of God you realize how insignificant racial differences really are. You become like children who have not yet learned to discriminate against others. I was only a child when I met my best friend Jackie Smith. When Jackie and her family began attending my father's church, we were both nine years old. Though we were too bashful to say hello, we stared at each other across the aisle week after week until our fathers finally introduced us at the end of a Sunday service. Two little girls, shy but curious, eager to make a new friend. The world may have viewed us as being different from one another, but that thought never crossed our minds. Our friendship clicked at that moment. It didn't matter to either of us that we were from different racial backgrounds. And it still doesn't matter more than forty years later.

Jackie knows me as well as anyone. She's been my prayer partner, my encourager, and nothing short of a sister to me. And she's been right beside me during all the difficult moments of my life. Her friendship without a doubt is one of God's greatest blessings to me. Wouldn't it be wonderful if we could all be as children, like Jackie and I the day we met, so open to others and not dwelling on differences? Our lives would be so much richer, even as rich as Jackie has made mine.

Both Jim and I have been grateful that God has placed us in the midst of so many different kinds of people. It's broadened us as people and as ministers of Jesus Christ because God has helped us to see people through his eyes.

Unfortunately, there have been times when visiting Christians have voiced comments that have been like arrows to our hearts. Their bigotry and narrowness have caused us tremendous grief. At the same time, some minority ministers have said nasty things to members of our congregation, criticizing them for attending a church where the choir director and the senior pastor are white. Racism is not a one-way street. No matter where it comes from, all of it grieves the heart of God and makes our preaching and singing about Jesus mere hypocrisy.

> *Racism is not a one-way street. No matter where it comes from, all of it grieves the heart of God and makes our preaching and singing about Jesus mere hypocrisy.*

Despite the blessing of a tightly knit spiritual family, a friend like Jackie, and a husband who has always supported me, I would be less than honest if I didn't tell you that there was a time when our unity was threatened by an attack of Satan. Life had become so difficult for me that I wanted to run as fast and as far away from Brooklyn as I could. I wanted to pack my bags, gather up my children, and drive away forever. I was more than ready to call it quits.

I WANT OUT

Jim, we can't stay here a minute longer. We've got to get out before it's too late. I'm leaving and taking the kids with me whether you come or not."

I wasn't kidding either. I was prepared to get in the car and drive away with two of my three children. It was 1988 and I'd had all I could take. I wasn't angry, just so scared and depressed that I could hardly pray. It felt like my world had come crashing in on me.

I had always known there would be challenges involved in an inner-city ministry. Nobody had to remind me. Not since the Sunday I sat at the organ watching a man walk down the aisle holding a gun in his hand. Jim couldn't hear my screams of warning because everyone was praying. And he couldn't see what was coming toward him because his eyes were closed.

I felt paralyzed, sure that the man was going to shoot Jim and then turn around and shoot me. What would happen to our children, to the church? Was this how our ministry would end? Fortunately, the man dropped the gun on the pulpit and collapsed in a heap sobbing. God had protected us once again, but I was angry with the ushers. How could they allow such a thing to happen? Why weren't they watching? Didn't

I felt paralyzed, sure that the man was going to shoot Jim and then turn around and shoot me. What would happen to our children, to the church? Was this how our ministry would end?

they know that anything could happen in the heart of downtown Brooklyn?

Still, I loved the work God had called us to even though I knew there were risks for both Jim and me. I was more than willing to meet the challenges, or so I thought. I just didn't bargain on my children being pulled away from God while we were giving ourselves to the ministry. That was more than I could bear.

HAD WE LOST OUR CHILD?

I'd always worried about my three children attending public schools in New York, but there was no money to send them to private schools. Surprisingly, the problem didn't begin in school. It started in church. Right under our noses.

Our oldest, Chrissy, had gotten involved with some unhealthy influences at the Brooklyn Tabernacle. Gradually, we began to see a hardening of her heart toward us and toward God. She changed from the sweet well-behaved youngster we had raised to someone we could hardly recognize. My husband has told the story from his perspective in his book *Fresh Wind, Fresh Fire*. From where I stood, it seemed as though she was being destroyed in front of our eyes. I felt helpless as she spun out of control.

Despite our pleading, Chrissy remained hard as a rock. My husband did most of the talking with her but got absolutely nowhere. Yelling, crying, encouragement, gifts, and a change of location—we tried it all. But she wouldn't budge. Eventually Chrissy left home, which was something we never dreamed could happen. The more we prayed, the worse she seemed to get. On and on it went until the pain of it for a mother's heart became excruciating.

One Friday night as the choir began to pray before practice, I felt so attacked by Satan that I thought I was losing my mind. The pressure was so strong that I did the unthinkable and just walked out of practice. Then I made my way to a local department store where I sat for two hours in the furniture section sobbing my heart out.

That night, it seemed as though Satan was whispering an ugly threat to me. He had gotten hold of Chrissy and he was going to devour Susan and James as well unless I got them out of New York. I loved my husband. I loved the choir and the work God had called us to. But I wasn't willing to sacrifice my children. I didn't know what to do.

I felt the weight of the last two years of Chrissy's rebellion pressing in on me. Had Jim and I overstayed our time in Brooklyn? Were we asking too much of ourselves and assuming it was God's will? If not, why had we lost our daughter? The questions kept swirling around me, eroding my faith. That was when I decided I had to do something. I wasn't going to lose my other two children the way I had lost Chrissy.

Still, I loved the work God had called us to even though I knew there were risks for both Jim and me. I just didn't bargain on my children being pulled away from God while we were giving ourselves to the ministry.

I loved my husband. I loved the choir and the work God had called us to. But I wasn't willing to sacrifice my children. I didn't know what to do.

When I told Jim I was ready to pack my bags and leave with the other two kids, he was stunned, "Carol, we can't just leave without knowing what God wants us to do. He's called us here. We have to hold on until he gives us clear direction."

Somehow I managed to resist the temptation to run, I don't know how, but I had a hard time keeping my anxiety and depression under control.

"WHAT IS WRONG WITH ME?"

Neither Jim nor I realized I was facing battles on more than one front. In fact I hadn't felt well for some time. It started right about the time Chrissy was having her own difficulties. At night I would lay in bed wondering what was wrong with me. Was the worry just eating me up or was it something else? Since I couldn't put my finger on anything specific, I did my best to ignore it. But one day as I walked into my office my assistant, Miriam Diaz, announced: "Carol, I made an appointment for you with my doctor in Manhattan."

"Why did you do that?" I asked her.

"You know you can't go on like this, Carol. You need to see a doctor."

Giving in to her gentle pressure, I kept the appointment and soon discovered the reason I'd been feeling so unwell. Tests revealed cancer cells in my body.

"We need to operate right away to keep it from spreading," the doctor told me. So I was scheduled for an immediate hysterectomy. Miriam had probably saved my life, though I didn't appreciate it at the time.

The Sunday night before my Monday morning surgery I was assigned to a room with three other beds in it. I felt frightened because I had no idea what the surgeon would find when he opened me up. Cancer had already taken my grandmother and some of my aunts and uncles. I couldn't help wondering if I was next.

The next evening as I was coming out from under the sedation, I heard the news: the surgery had gone well. The doctors believed they had succeeded in rooting out the cancer from my body. But the news didn't cheer me as it should have. And as I lay in bed, it seemed like different storm fronts were suddenly converging on me—physical pain, a deep sense of hopelessness and isolation, and fear about the future. I struggled to keep my head above the churning waters.

As I lay in bed, it seemed like different storm fronts were suddenly converging on me—physical pain, a deep sense of hopelessness and isolation, and fear about the future. I struggled to keep my head above the churning waters.

I rang for the nurse repeatedly, thinking that if only she would give me something to alleviate the pain then perhaps I could sleep. But she never came, and this heightened my anguish even more. No one seemed able to help me. I lay awake, unable to chase away the darkness that had settled over me.

Then, at about 3:00 A.M., I heard a slight shuffling sound outside the curtain drawn around my bed. Suddenly, a woman appeared at the foot of my bed with a Bible in her hand. I had never seen her before, but I felt no alarm as she began gently rubbing my legs while she prayed in Spanish. Though I couldn't understand the words she was speaking, I knew she was holding me before the throne of grace. I had felt so alone and now it was as though God had sent one of his servants to help me and assure me he was near. Soothed by her prayers, I fell asleep.

The next morning I learned that this woman had been assigned to one of the other beds in my room. Though she couldn't speak a word of English, her daughter told me that she had been hospitalized with varicose veins so painful she could hardly stand. I don't know how she managed to walk over to my bed and stand there praying in the middle of the night. It was purely an act of the Holy Spirit.

THE GIFT OF A SONG

The next day nothing had changed, at least not outwardly. I was still in a great deal of pain from the surgery. But I felt a sense of peace I hadn't known for some time. God had chosen a complete stranger to assure me that he was aware of everything I was going through. My nighttime visitor had succeeded in reminding me that I wasn't alone. That was when the Lord sent a special song into my soul. The words of the chorus came to me immediately, as I lay there in bed.

> In my moment of fear
> Through every pain, every tear
> There's a God Who's been faithful to me.
> When my strength was all gone,
> When my heart had no song,
> Still in love He's proved faithful to me.
> Every word He's promised is true;
> What I thought was impossible I see my God do.

> *Chorus:*
> He's been faithful, faithful to me.
> Looking back His loving mercy I see
> Though in my heart I have questioned
> Even failed to believe
> Yet He's been faithful, faithful to me.

> When my heart looked away,
> The many times I could not pray
> Still my God He was faithful to me.
> The days I spent so selfishly,

Reaching out for what pleased me;
Even then God was faithful to me.
Every time I come back to Him,
He is waiting with open arms
And I see once again.

Chorus:
He's been faithful, faithful to me.
Looking back His loving mercy I see
Though in my heart I have questioned
Even failed to believe
Yet He's been faithful, faithful to me.

Though I didn't have a piano to work out the music, it didn't matter. I held the song close to me until I was well enough to write out the words and the music.

After my release, I still had more battles ahead of me. But now my faith was being renewed. The song the Lord gave me became like a balm to my heart, strengthening me once again. Though I didn't know it at the time, "He's Been Faithful" is the song that would have a greater impact than any I had ever written, blessing people across the country and throughout the world. Someone once told my husband, that this song was like an anchor holding them in place when everything around them was falling apart. It was a song of hope born in the midst of my pain.

A FATHER'S PAIN

During my time of struggle, Jim was as broken up by Chrissy's condition as I was, but he reacted differently. At first he confided in some close friends, but after a few months he sensed God wanting him, as he says, "to stop crying, screaming, or talking to anyone else about Chrissy. I was to converse with no one but God." That meant keeping Chrissy at a distance too, and though it broke my heart that the two of them weren't talking to each other, I knew I had to respect his decision. One Tuesday night Jim headed to the prayer meeting, his heart still heavy with the knowledge that Chrissy was so far from God. He tells what happened:

"An usher handed me a note. A young woman whom I felt to be spiritually sensitive had written: *Pastor Cymbala, I feel impressed that we should stop the meeting and all pray for your daughter.*

"I hesitated. Was it right to change the flow of the service and focus on my personal need?

"Yet something in the note seemed to ring true. In a few minutes I picked up a microphone and told the congregation what had just happened. 'The truth of the matter,' I said, 'although I haven't talked much about it, is that my daughter is very far from God these days. She thinks up is down and down is up; dark is light, and light is dark. But I know God can break through to her, and so I'm going to ask Pastor Boekstaaf to lead us in praying for Chrissy.'" [1]

It was almost as though the church experienced labor pains that night as they prayed God would bring our daughter from death to life. When Jim came home from the prayer meeting he told me, "Carol, it's over."

"What's over?" I asked him.

"It's over with Chrissy. You would have had to be in the prayer meeting tonight to understand, but I tell you, if there's a God in heaven, this whole nightmare is finally over."

That evening, though we didn't know it, Chrissy was having her own nightmare. She woke up frightened by a terrible

[1]Jim Cymbala, *Fresh Wind, Fresh Fire* (Grand Rapids: Zondervan, 1997), pp. 63–64.

dream. In it, she could see herself heading toward a bottomless pit. She felt terrified, realizing her sin was leading her straight to hell. But as she dreamed, she also felt God holding her back from the edge and lifting her up. In the midst of her fear, he was telling her how much he loved her.

I could hardly believe it when I opened the door on Thursday morning and saw her standing there. She actually fell on her knees and began begging our forgiveness for how she had been living. I threw my arms around her and we both burst into tears. I had my child back at last.

Our nightmare had lasted two years. They had seemed the worst years of our lives, and I had nearly lost the struggle because of my fear for my children. But God had not abandoned us. Instead he had shown his faithfulness in a marvelous way. And Chrissy's life was beginning all over again.

A FUTURE FULL OF HOPE

A few months later my husband and I were astonished when a Bible school in the northeast invited our twenty-year-old daughter to lead their choir and help direct the music program. Chrissy had simply been inquiring about taking a few classes, but the school's administrators felt that God had sent her as an answer to prayer. When they asked us what we thought of the possibility, Jim told them that Chrissy had never led any kind of singing group before and that she could neither read nor write music. But that didn't discourage them. They simply promised to pack their choral books away so that she could teach the students by rote. That's how Chrissy began directing choirs exactly like her mother!

Before long she fell in love with a wonderful young man by the name of Al Toledo. Al's family had emigrated from Cuba, and he had grown up in Brooklyn. A major league baseball prospect before injuring himself in college sports, Al had grown close to the Lord while attending the Brooklyn

Tabernacle. Before long Al and Chrissy were married and the Lord called them both into ministry. After serving the Lord in Rhode Island and New Jersey, Al became the pastor of a church in Nebraska, while Chrissy served as its choir director. Two years ago they joined the staff at our church, providing tremendous support for Jim and me. Now we are able to enjoy our three grandchildren whenever we like.

When Chrissy was going through her time of difficulty, I worried about what might happen to my other two children. When you are in ministry you make certain sacrifices that also affect your children. Would the devil take them as well, I fretted. Though Jim and I did our best to provide the kind of loving home they needed, I knew that each of my children had paid a price for the work we were doing in the church. Because of all the demands on us, we certainly weren't your typical all-American family. But God kept them from harm. Susan is now the mother of two children and a soloist in the choir who regularly leads worship during the Sunday services. Her husband, Brian Pettrey, is a graduate of the Virginia Military Institute and a man with an intense love for Jesus.

When I stand in front of the choir, I also have the pleasure of looking up into the tenor section and seeing another member of my family. No one puts more heart and effort into his singing than my son, James, who has been gifted with a wonderful voice. Three children all serving the Lord, not only safe in his keeping but living their lives in a way that will bless others. When I look at what God has done to save so many broken people through the ministry of the church, I know that my children have played an important role in the story.

I wish I could tell you that our nightmare with our daughter was something unusual, something you will never need to face in your own family. But you know as well as I that similar struggles are being played out every day in families across the country. Perhaps you have seen your own children sliding away from you an inch at a time, or maybe you feel you lost them years ago. If you have faced such a challenge in your own family, your faith may be under assault as mine was. Though I can hardly set myself up as a shining example of how to respond when something like this happens, I can honestly point to the shining example of how God was faithful. I can also tell you from painful experience that the very worst thing you can do when your children or someone you love is in trouble is to begin doubting God's power or his desire to save them. Believe me, he has not forgotten our situation or us. He has promised to hold our hand as we stand on his promise to recover the precious property that Satan has tried to steal.

If we are going to fight, our battle can only be won through prayer. We must draw closer than ever to God, believing in his faithfulness. "Call upon me in the day of trouble; I will deliver you" (Psalm 50:15)—these are not empty words but a clear promise from Almighty God. Throughout the struggle, however long or short it may last; we will certainly be attacked by confusion. We will be tempted to give up. But just as God gave me the grace to stay, even when I wanted to run, he will give you the grace to do whatever it takes to fight for your children.

In ways you cannot possibly imagine, God will use the very attack of Satan on your children's lives to accomplish great things for his glory. Don't let the circumstances fool you. Don't let your faith be shaken. God's love is so powerful it can touch any heart, even the heart that seems impossibly far from him.

TEN

FIGHTING FOR THE PROMISE

The early days of our ministry often felt bumpy, as though we were driving too fast down a dirt road in the middle of the night with only one headlight. We couldn't see very far in front of us, and we never knew what we might run into. Some nights, while I was at home with the kids, Jim would call from church to tell me about the latest challenge.

I'll never forget Austin, a huge guy we inherited as a regular visitor when we first came to the Brooklyn Tabernacle. One day he made a vulgar remark to a woman in the church, frightening her and angering her husband. Jim tried to head off a nasty scene by warning Austin over the phone. But Austin, a very troubled person, exploded, telling my husband, "I'm coming over there tonight with my boys, and we're going to mess you up, preacher."

"Listen," Jim replied, "you might very well mess me up, but I know you well enough to know you don't have any boys coming with you."

That night Jim was leading the tiny midweek service so he warned a young man to keep an eye on the door for Austin. Sure enough, while the small group was praying, Austin came barging in, all 250 pounds of him, demanding to see "the preacher." Jim went to the back of the church to try and calm him while someone else called the police. As soon as Austin saw him he started cursing and threatening, but before he could do anything the police burst through the door, nightsticks in hand. Jim wouldn't press charges so they eventually released Austin, but not before cracking him across the back of the knees and frisking him. Later that night, Jim received a phone call as he was leaving the church.

"Okay, I didn't do it tonight, but I will get you next week for sure," Austin promised. Fortunately, he never came back. Austin was one more bump in the very rough road we were traveling.

Jim didn't tell me about Austin until it was all over. But I knew his life could be threatened at any moment, and such knowledge hardly left me at ease. Rather than living in a constant state of worry, however, I decided to trust God, believing that he was our ultimate protection in the midst of the dangers we faced.

Moments like these were not confined to the early years of our ministry. A few years ago, a strange looking man walked up to the platform at the end of a service. He was smiling as he shook my hand, gripping it so tightly I realized he was trying to break it. When I cried out, he calmly turned and walked away. Later I learned that he had just tried the same maneuver on my husband. The man looked like a bodybuilder and wore a tight black T-shirt that said "Gold's Gym" across the front. I guess he had decided to practice his workout regimen in the sanctuary that day.

One time, as I was saying good-bye to my ninety-six-year-old grandmother, a woman ran at me outside of church. She slapped me full force across the side of my face knocking off my earring and nearly pushing me to the ground. Apparently she had been forcibly removed from the building because of an earlier disturbance. As soon as the ushers relaxed their grip, she saw me and something triggered another violent reaction. Hours later I could still see the angry red welt on my face.

SPIRITUAL PROTECTION

I have little doubt that some of these attacks are demonically inspired. How else can you explain them? Still, God's protection has been incredible. With all the ways the enemy has tried to interfere, an aching hand or a sore face is all that he's managed to accomplish.

The truth is that when you're doing what God wants and going where he wants you to go, there's a spiritual umbrella of protection over your head. But that umbrella doesn't follow you. Instead, you have to follow it. When the Israelites left Egypt for the Promised Land, they didn't go out alone. God's presence went before them into the desert in the form of a cloud. Whenever the cloud lifted, they broke camp. Whenever it settled in, they pitched camp. Even when they finally reached the Promised Land, they didn't just walk in and settle down. No, they had to fight to take the land. But God cared for them and gave them the victory.

In much the same way, I know I need to stay close to God and then fight for the promises he has given. When I am doing his will I can depend on his help. But I can only take the land God wants to give me, just as the Israelites could only take the land God had promised them. If I attempt to do something God isn't asking me to or if I try

> *The truth is that when you're doing what God wants and going where he wants you to go, there's a spiritual umbrella of protection over your head. But that umbrella doesn't follow you. Instead, you have to follow it.*

to fulfill his promises on my terms, then I will never receive the full blessing he has for my life.

A BIZARRE ATTACK

One of the strangest spiritual attacks we ever encountered took place soon after Jim and I began serving at the Brooklyn Tabernacle. We were living in New Jersey when we got a call late one Sunday night from a pastor from South Dakota. I'm not sure how he heard about the church, but he said he and his wife had been praying about coming to New York City. Jim didn't know them and said little, but the next Sunday night they called again telling us they felt led by God to come to Brooklyn to help out. Jim assured them we had no money for additional staff members but said that if they wanted to come and attend church for a while they were of course free to do so.

At that time we were still living in a house in New Jersey for which Jim's parents had provided the down payment. To make ends meet while we were pastoring both churches, I worked a job at a local high school cafeteria while Jim did some coaching on the side. The night the couple arrived from South Dakota, we welcomed them into our home and served them the best dinner we could afford—chuck steaks, green beans, mashed potatoes, and dessert. They seemed nice and as poor as we were.

After dinner, Jim drove them into Brooklyn and settled them into a little apartment over the church because they had no place to go. A few days later we got a phone call from a woman who lived in an adjacent apartment. "Pastor, do you know what these people are saying about you?" she asked. "They've been telling folks you don't care about the people in the church. They say you've been living it up with big steak dinners at the church's expense. And there's a lot of other crazy stuff. I think you better talk to them right away."

When Jim hung up the phone, he had no idea that this was the beginning of one of the strongest and strangest demonic attacks we ever encountered, as though someone was trying to kill the church while it was still young and vulnerable. Though Jim doesn't like to talk about it, he remembers it well.

"It was a Monday evening when I received the phone call warning me of the trouble at church. At first I didn't take it too seriously but something strange happened as I began reading my Bible. A tremendous spirit of prayer came over me and I could not stop praying. Carol was asleep upstairs, and after a while I began pacing around the house praying out loud. My heart was filled with an unusual sense of spiritual tension. It seemed as if the Holy Spirit was preparing me for something, though I didn't know what. This went on for hours until I became so stirred in my heart that I knew I wouldn't be able to sleep.

"At 2:30 A.M. I finally decided to drive into Brooklyn and catch a little rest before starting work in the morning. I left Carol a note and headed off in my car. But even as I drove in toward the Holland Tunnel, I kept praying, crying out to God for his grace and power.

"I knocked on the door of the church apartment about 9:00 A.M., and the couple from South Dakota invited me in for a cup of coffee. As we sat chatting at the kitchen table, I introduced the subject that was now heavy on my heart. I confronted them with the reports I had received and asked for an explanation. What happened next was like something out of a horror movie.

"The man stared at his wife oddly, ignoring my question. Then he smiled and said, 'Maybe we should tell him now, honey, right?' Then a smile spread across her face as well, and she let out a low, eerie laugh that made my flesh crawl. They both turned on me at once and the man said: 'You're through here. This isn't your church anymore. We're taking over, so get out!'

"What had happened to the nice young couple Carol and I had hosted just a few days earlier? They had seemed so shy and sweet. Now they were staring at me and snarling, telling me to leave the church or else. I was so shocked by the change in their personalities that I was speechless for a moment. Then I began trying to reason with them but that only seemed to incense them further. They got up and started circling the room.

"I had grown up playing basketball in the playgrounds of the city. I knew about shoving, elbowing, and other rough stuff from the basketball court. But this was a fight of another kind, of another dimension.

I had grown up playing basketball in the playgrounds of the city. I knew about shoving, elbowing, and other rough stuff from the basketball court. But this was a fight of another kind, of another dimension.

"Foolishly I kept trying to reason with them, but they would have none of it. They kept declaring that they were taking over then and there, and I better accept it. It went on like that for hours. As we argued they kept glancing at each other, making those low, eerie laughing sounds.

"The more they laughed, the more I prayed, asking God to show me what to do. Suddenly I stopped trying to reason with them and blurted out, 'That's it. No more. Get out of this building right now or I'll . . . I'll—call the police!' I couldn't believe what I was saying. What an insane situation!

"That's when they told me that an elderly woman who had lent the previous pastor $15,000 to help buy the little building now wanted all her money back. They had shared their 'spiritual revelations' with her, slandering Carol and me in the process, and now this woman was going to a lawyer to recover the loan.

"That was it. I got so angry about how they were undermining the church that I ordered them once and for all to pack up and leave the building. By then, the man was standing about fifteen feet away. Suddenly he gave out a yell and started running straight at me as if to hit me! I had only a second to react but God helped me. Instead of following my natural instinct, which would have been to grab him and throw him out the second-floor window, I just closed my eyes and waited for the impact. It never came. He stopped inches away, with a furious look on his face.

"After that the couple suddenly changed tactics. Their bizarre responses were perfectly synchronized. Now they couldn't be nice enough, couldn't apologize enough. They were so sorry. Could they just stay a night or two longer? Could they find another way to help us in the ministry? But I knew that even one more day of these two would bring irreparable harm to our little church.

"Finally, at about 4:30 P.M., after a day of wrangling, they drove off. I watched from the second-floor window, fighting back tears. Though I was young and physically strong, I was so exhausted that it took me a solid week to recover. I spent most of my time laid out on the couch, as though I'd just gone the full fifteen rounds in a heavyweight fight."

This strange encounter stunned both Jim and me. We felt knocked down but not knocked out because we knew that the work God had begun in the church was precious. Why else would the enemy go to such lengths to try to destroy us?

WE SHOULDN'T BE SURPRISED

Though this attempted hijacking of our small church was the most bizarre attack we ever faced, we knew that spiritual warfare came with the territory. It was part of the cost of doing God's work. I'd seen this kind of opposition often enough, growing up in my father's church. If you were going to serve God, you were also going to encounter difficulty.

Christians who are fighting God's battles will be very familiar with the fierce onslaughts and subtle strategies of the enemy. That is why the Bible commands us to "be strong in the Lord and in his mighty power. Put on the full armor of God so that you can take your stand against the devil's schemes. For our struggle is not against flesh and blood, but against the rulers, against the authorities, against the powers of this dark world and against the spiritual forces of evil in the heavenly realms" (Ephesians 6:10–12). It's evident from God's Word that serving Jesus means confronting powerful forces of spiritual darkness, but these will always be conquered through the greater power of the Holy Spirit as we trust in Christ.

Many of Satan's attacks are much more subtle than the ones I've described. Though less obvious, these can still be effective attempts to discourage or sidetrack us. Whenever, for instance, I have set myself to write new songs, lay down rhythm tracks, or record the choir singing, there have been spiritual onslaughts that only God's grace has helped me face. That's been true with every one of the more than twenty projects I've recorded.

One time the choir was recording a live album that was to be taped during the Sunday afternoon and evening services. It was a steamy summer day, and an expensive recording truck was parked outside the church, hooked up to all the sound microphones in the sanctuary. The building was packed when suddenly someone spotted smoke near the ceiling of the auditorium. Fortunately no one panicked as we evacuated the congregation. In a few minutes, the fire department arrived with axes in hand while two thousand people waited outside on two different streets. As we stood there, I couldn't help wondering whether we would have to abandon the recording. If we didn't tape the album that day there would be the additional expense of hiring another remote truck, and I didn't think we could afford it.

As firemen spread out through the building searching for the cause of the smoke, I was surprised to hear exuberant singing outside on Park Place. It was the congregation, not the choir, and they were singing "Let God Arise and His Enemies Be Scattered." The same thing was happening on Flatbush Avenue. People sang and clapped their hands with no musical accompaniment but it was some of the sweetest singing I had ever heard.

As I listened, I was filled with faith. Satan was trying to interrupt whatever God intended to do through this new album. But we weren't cooperating with his plans. If anything, I now felt a new excitement to record the album.

To our relief the building wasn't on fire. It had simply been a burned out fan in the exhaust system. After an okay from the fire marshals, everyone re-entered the church and the meeting continued as if nothing had happened. With 90° temperatures outside and smoke inside, that album turned out to be one of the hottest recordings we ever made!

Neither the congregation nor the choir was surprised that the little problem with the fan happened on that particular Sunday. Because of how Satan works, we have learned to expect distractions, discouragement, and disappointments whenever we reach out to others in Christ's name. If the apostle Paul went through hardships, beatings, and imprisonment doing God's work, we know we will sooner or later encounter our own set of difficulties. We are convinced that spiritual warfare is real and that the same sensitivity of spirit that helps us follow God's leadings will also alert us to satanic attacks.

A STORYBOOK OF GRACE

When it comes to opposition, there's no battle more fiercely fought than the one for our souls. In the end, that's what spiritual opposition is all about—keeping us separated from the God who loves us. Sometimes the struggle is subtle, but often it's an all out war, as in the case of a young woman who's been part of the choir for the last three years. Victoria Council calls her life a storybook of God's grace even though her early years don't read anything like a storybook. If anything, the plot seemed to have been scripted by someone who intended to crush her young life before it had a chance to begin.

"My parents moved to New York in 1953. They lived together for thirteen years before getting married, probably because my father had already been married twice before, with plenty of children back in Puerto Rico to prove it. Together they had six more children, and I was the baby of the family.

"We lived in an apartment on the fifth floor of a housing project near the Brooklyn Navy Yard, and neither of my parents worked because my mother stayed home to take care of the kids and my father collected disability pay from an injury he had while working as a painter.

"When my mother discovered she was pregnant with me, she was anything but happy. She knew my father already felt trapped and boxed in, forced to care for a wife and five children when all he wanted to do was drink and play his violin.

"As time went on, my father's anger got so bad that he began beating my mother as well as my brothers and sisters.

He kept a belt by the door so he could hit them with the buckle end whenever they came home late. No wonder my siblings retaliated by staying out even later, drinking, and taking drugs to numb the pain of growing up in a home like ours.

"My mother did her best to defend her children even though her protests meant getting her hair pulled out and being beaten over the head with a frying pan. But no matter what she did, she saw her children slipping away from her one by one.

"As the youngest, I watched the nightmare unfolding—my alcoholic father unable to control his anger, my mother so bullied she became a woman with no voice or opinion, and my siblings so hurt that they turned to drugs and alcohol. I watched as they shot up heroin and began stealing to feed their habits and then as they marched off to prison. I decided I would never touch drugs or alcohol after seeing how it was destroying them. Still, I was a frightened child who thought surely she was going to lose her mind.

"Everyone said I was my father's favorite, but that brought such confusion to my heart because even a little girl knows that when someone loves you they take care of you. They don't hurt you. Unfortunately, I slept in a small bed in my parents' room because the apartment was so crowded. My father made a habit of sending my mother to the store so that he and I would be left alone together. That's when the sexual abuse began. I was four years old.

"The abuse went on for several years, long enough to warp my perception of love. Having friends was impossible because I didn't even like myself. And kids at school made fun of me because, like my mother, I had no voice and couldn't stand up for myself.

"Believe it or not, while all this was going on at home, we had been going to church. I made my first communion, attended confirmation classes, and went to Mass every Sunday. I knew how to pray. And I did every night, begging that God would keep me safe and help my family. But the older I got the more I began to wonder where God was in the midst of all my troubles.

"Things got easier by the time I went to high school. I liked my classes, and though I still stayed pretty much to myself, I had a few friends. By then all my siblings had moved out of the house. I'll never forget the day I heard the news that three of them had already contracted the AIDS virus. I was so upset, so angry with them for destroying their lives. But I was even angrier with God for putting me into a family that was so messed up.

"Before long I met a boy I absolutely adored, and we moved to Albany. But he was flawed like all my former boyfriends. Soon enough he got hooked on crack. One day he asked me, the girl who never drank or did drugs, to sample something that looked like a cigarette. I hesitated but began inhaling it. Before long I started hallucinating and ended up in the hospital. I remember wondering if this was how things were going to end. But God had other plans.

"Despite the fact that my life was a mess, I still wanted to improve it. But every time I tried, something happened to ruin things. Still I was determined to get ahead and made arrangements to attend college. By now my father, disliking the cold weather, was spending the winters in Puerto Rico while my mother was living in New York. One winter we heard the news that he had fallen ill. Before long we heard more news. My father had died, but not before marrying again in Puerto Rico, even though he was still married to my mother.

"It was hard to mourn the man who had wreaked so much havoc in our family. Even in death he seemed to control my life. Suddenly my plans for college had to be put on hold because my mother needed help with the bills and the house. I started feeling bitter, sure that no matter how hard I tried, I would never be able to move forward with my life.

"I didn't realize that things were about to get a whole lot worse. I met a man I had known years earlier in our old neighborhood. Though he had just finished serving time in prison, he seemed to have his life back on track. Before long we moved into an apartment around the corner from the Brooklyn Tabernacle. But something wasn't quite right. I noticed that he always seemed sweaty and tired. He would often fall asleep while I was talking. But when I asked him about it he told me it was because he was working so hard, and I believed him.

"Despite his strange behaviors, he seemed to have a strong belief in God, and I found his faith inspiring, at least at first. Then we went to Puerto Rico to visit his mother, and he took me to visit a woman who also claimed to love the Lord. As soon as she saw me, she took my hand and tried to read my future. As she did, she wrote things on pieces of paper and then placed them in oil. When we returned to New York, we were to put them in special places. This would bring me some kind of blessing.

"When we got home, I discovered my boyfriend had placed these notes in little bottles and hidden them everywhere—in the freezer, under the bed, in all the cabinets. Meanwhile, his beeper kept going off at all hours of the night and he always seemed sick. I knew something strange was going on but didn't know what it was, and I no longer trusted him.

"As crazy as things were, we decided to get married. My mother was happy that I had found someone but worried because she saw that we were tearing each other apart, arguing as we tried to plan the wedding.

"And I felt increasingly uncomfortable in our apartment, as though we were no longer alone. Someone or something had followed us back from Puerto Rico, something I couldn't see but whose power I could certainly sense.

"Even though I had a great job and was planning to be married, I began to feel depressed. A darkness was creeping over me that I couldn't shake. Then, shortly before the wedding, I discovered that my future husband, the man I loved, was hooked on heroin. No wonder he had always been falling asleep. No wonder he was sick all the time. He tried so hard to keep the truth from me but the drug withdrawal symptoms were unmistakable.

"My fiancé ended up back in prison, and I stayed on alone in the apartment. I had no plans. No future. No hope. It seemed like a struggle even to breathe. Nearly everyone important to me had been addicted to drugs or alcohol. My three siblings were diagnosed with AIDS and now my wedding was destroyed. It felt like a set up, like someone was trying to crush the life out of me. I wanted to die.

I felt increasingly uncomfortable in our apartment, as though we were no longer alone. Someone or something had followed us back from Puerto Rico, something I couldn't see but whose power I could certainly sense.

"My mother urged me to go to church, but I would just tell her, 'I don't need to go to church. I can pray at home.' But I couldn't because everything seemed so dark and hopeless.

"So I decided to end my life. But before I figured out how to do it, I suddenly thought about the church around the corner from where I lived. I had passed it many times but had never gone in. Now something seemed to be urging me there, as though it was a place I could go and give my wounded heart a touch of life again. So in December of

1995 I crawled into the Brooklyn Tabernacle without much more than a shred of hope. Through the prayer and the singing and the preaching I had such a sense of God loving me and drawing me that I gave myself to him right then. I felt as though he was telling me he wanted to bring the little girl who had gone into hiding out into the light again so that he could reveal himself to her.

"The darkness in my life suddenly lifted. I moved out of the apartment and as time went on I began to experience God touching parts of me that had seemed beyond repair, telling me with the words of the Bible that 'he had always known the plans he had for me, plans to prosper me, and not to harm me, plans to give me a future and a hope.'

"As I think about my life, I realize that Satan had always planned to destroy me. He thought he could crush me with violence, abuse, and addiction and even with the occult. And his plan almost worked. I had been ready to take my life.

"But God had a plan too, and he had been working it out from the very beginning, though I couldn't see it at the time. He had heard the lonely prayers of a little girl afraid in her bed. He had kept my mind sound enough to hear him calling me by my name. And he had protected me from being destroyed by drugs and alcohol even though I'd been surrounded by them all my life.

"That's why I can say that my life is a storybook of God's grace. Because whatever Satan meant for evil, God ultimately used for good. When I read the words of Psalm 139 I know they apply to me: 'For you created my inmost being; you knit me together in my mother's womb. I praise you because I am fearfully and wonderfully made; your works are wonderful, I know that full well. My frame was not hidden from you when I was made in the secret place. When I was woven together in the depths of the earth, your eyes saw my unformed body. All the days ordained for me were written in your book before one of them came to be.'

"Fifteen years later, my brothers and sisters who contracted the AIDS virus are still alive, and I now have the confidence I need to speak to them about God's love. Today I am not afraid to say it straight out: God's light is more powerful than the darkest secret in any of our lives."

Victoria Council knows all too well of the reality of evil. She knows that Satan's power is at work seeking to destroy lives. Because of his attacks she nearly ended her own life. But instead, because of God's far greater power, she is very much alive. Today she is married to a wonderful husband who stands with her on the platform every Sunday, worshiping the One who has filled her with hope and shown her his plan for her life.

As Christians, we cannot hide from the battle, nor should we fear it. It is simply a part of the life of faith. If you want to know God, to experience his blessing and be used by him, you will encounter opposition. But we are never alone in the struggle. Instead, God is with us, leading the way and keeping us safe.

ELEVEN

HE'S BEEN FAITHFUL

Following God is not always a smooth path. Sometimes the road is level and easy to walk. But more frequently, it's uphill and rocky with all kinds of challenges. Even in the early days, I often found myself in difficult situations.

I remember visiting a church in St. Louis, Missouri, shortly after Jim and I were married. During the service the minister surprised me by announcing to the three hundred people who were present that the Reverend Clair Hutchins's daughter was in the congregation. Would she please, he asked, come up and play during the offering? Silence. Again he pleaded, "Would Carol Cymbala please come up." More silence. Finally I managed to stand and in a quivering voice announce that I just didn't do those kinds of things. No amount of pleading could get me to budge from my seat that day.

Jim and I laugh when we recall stories like these because they remind us of how far I've come and just how much God has accomplished despite my initial timidity. They also remind me of a story in the Gospels that has always carried special meaning for me. It takes place in a synagogue, where Jesus met a man who suffered the deformity of a shriveled hand. Despite the objections of some of the Jews, scandalized that he would heal a man on the Sabbath, Jesus simply said to the man: "Stretch out your hand" (Mark 3:5). The man obviously understood the faith Jesus was asking him to exercise. Since one of his hands was healthy, he could simply have stretched out that hand toward the Lord. It was something he could have done naturally without help from anyone. But Jesus was asking him to do what *he couldn't normally do*—stretch out a withered hand by faith. He had to believe that as he obeyed the Lord's command to stretch out his shriveled hand, the power of Jesus was enough to make him whole. It was as he obeyed the word of the Lord that he found his miracle and experienced the power of Christ.

That man with the withered hand reminds me of myself and the way God has always worked in my life, asking me to do what I am not naturally able to do. When I have responded in faith, I have found that I can do all things through Christ. Truthfully, this is how God works in all our lives, asking us to do things that can only be done by the power of the Holy Spirit. To follow God involves a continual breaking, a saying no to our natural instinct to shrink back from challenges so that we can say yes to God's power at work through us. That's where the joy comes from—being filled with God and used for his glory.

I have come to realize that many of us make life with God so complicated, when it's really so simple. The truth is that God will show us his power if we simply trust him to do what he said he will. His power not only sets us free but also keeps us safe in the middle of the most difficult circumstances.

GOD'S KEEPING POWER

Kevin Lewis is a soloist for the choir and the administrator of the music department at the Brooklyn Tabernacle. When I look at this strapping six-foot-one-inch-tall young man, I find it hard to believe he was ever small enough to be held in his mother's arms. But it doesn't seem all that long ago that Jim held him up before the congregation, dedicating him to the Lord when he was just an infant.

A few years ago, Kevin attended a large high school, whose roster of famous graduates includes Barbara Streisand, Beverly Sills, Mickey Spillane, and Bobby Fischer. My husband graduated from the same school more than thirty-five years ago. But neither Jim nor any of these people would recognize Erasmus Hall High School today because Brooklyn's oldest high school has also become one of its most notorious, a place where reporters posing as students discovered it was easier to score a line of crack cocaine than borrow a pencil to write with.

Kevin was always a good kid, hanging around the music department after school, helping out with whatever he could. A member of the youth choir at church, he had been named the best male vocalist in his school two years running. Still, we knew it wasn't easy for him at Erasmus. But we didn't realize how hard it had been until he told us his story one day.

"I grew up at the Brooklyn Tabernacle, coming through the children's ministry, the youth ministry, and then the youth choir. During that time I was always the choir's biggest fan. I used to listen to their albums, mimicking the singers, always pestering my mother to buy the latest tape or get tickets to every outside concert.

"When I was twelve or thirteen I started wondering if I was missing out on something. Everyone but me seemed to be going out to parties and having a lot of fun.

"After junior high I planned on attending Tilden High School along with the rest of my friends. But one day I got a card in the mail announcing that I'd been accepted into Erasmus Hall High School's academy of arts program, considered one of the best in New York. I couldn't believe it. I had never applied to the program, didn't want to pursue a musical career, and definitely did not want to attend that school. Despite the reputation of its music program, it was one of the most dangerous schools in Brooklyn. It didn't help that none of my friends would be there either.

"My mother was as upset by the news as I was, so she tried to get me transferred. But school officials said it was such a tough program to get into that I would need to try it out for at least six months before making a transfer. Six months became four years for me.

"Erasmus High isn't your average school. One of the biggest in Brooklyn, it has a campus that sprawls across four city blocks. During my time there, the buildings were in such bad shape that if it was raining outside it was raining inside. Sometimes kids had to eat lunch with umbrellas over their heads because it was raining so hard in the lunchroom. As for me, I only went to the lunchroom once because it was so chaotic. While music blared in the background, kids just went on about their business, smoking and fighting. It was a good place to get robbed.

"Gym class wasn't much fun either because the locker room was filthy and there were mice running around everywhere. I remember telling one of my gym teachers that I didn't want to change my clothes for class. He just wrote me off, telling me I would fail the course if I didn't. So I went

> *Erasmus High isn't your average school. During my time there, the buildings were in such bad shape that if it was raining outside it was raining inside. Sometimes kids had to eat lunch with umbrellas over their heads because it was raining so hard in the lunchroom.*

ahead and changed, stuffing all my things into a locker. But when I came back, sure enough, the lock was broken and everything was gone.

"The bathrooms were even worse. Besides being filthy, they were where kids went to buy drugs. Everybody knew you could get marijuana in the third-floor bathroom of the science house. But you could also get arrested by policemen who patrolled the building. If a few guys were smoking joints when the cops strolled in, everybody would get busted. So a lot of kids avoided the bathrooms, preferring to urinate in the stairwells. I even saw feces on the steps sometimes as I headed up to class. The truth is you could do whatever you wanted on those steps. Some people even had sex there.

"There were also rapes and slashings. One day a kid got stabbed and died. After that, going to school became more like going to jail. Full-body searches, metal detectors, and ID cards were part of the daily drill. Sometimes it took thirty minutes just to get inside the building. You felt like a criminal even though you had done nothing wrong. And it still wasn't safe because kids would sell their ID cards to people who wanted access to the school.

"It wasn't always easy to get out either because the principal would occasionally announce over the loudspeaker system that nobody was to leave the building. It didn't matter that classes had ended at 2:00. Sometimes we stayed until 4:00 because of gang violence that was happening outside the building. One thing I never did was go to school on Halloween because as far as I was concerned that was the devil's holiday, a day for gang initiations, a day when anything might happen.

"But except for getting robbed a few times, I never really had a problem. If I saw trouble coming toward me I would just walk the other way. I kept pretty much to myself so people didn't mess with me. Some kids may even have been a little afraid of me because they didn't know what I was thinking, didn't know what to expect. Big as I am, they didn't realize that I was the biggest chicken around.

"Meanwhile, some of my friends at Tilden High School weren't faring too well. Most of them were good kids who fell in with a bad crowd and then started going down the wrong road. One of them ended up in jail. Another dropped out of sight for two weeks. He turned up in a backyard in Queens. Apparently he got into some kind of trouble with the police, got shot, and then went into somebody's yard and bled to death.

"But the worst thing of all happened to my friend Shondell two months after she went off to Tilden High and I went on to Erasmus. She and I had always been close. I liked her but she was tough, so tough that nobody could beat her up, at least that's what I thought. So I couldn't believe it when I heard she'd been attacked at a party by girls she'd fought with three years earlier. It was a Saturday night when the girls got hold of her. They stabbed her over and over, seventeen times. Two sisters ended up in jail for her murder.

"My mother and my aunt went to the funeral home with me because Shondell had been a friend of the family. The night we went the place was packed with junior high and high school kids. We were all sitting down in the funeral parlor when everything exploded around us. Bullets started flying everywhere, and people scattered as fast as they could. My mother and I dove under the nearest pew while my aunt ran downstairs and hid in the casket showroom. By the time it was all over a couple of people had been grazed by bullets, and Shondell's casket was riddled with holes. It seems that family members of the two girls who had killed her stopped by to pay their respects. They shot up the place to retaliate for the fact that the two sisters had been arrested.

"All these things happened the first year I was at Erasmus. After that I realized I wasn't missing out on anything my old friends were doing out there in the world. If Shondell could die, anything could happen.

"Strange as it sounds, I began to realize that God had actually been protecting me by sending me to Erasmus High. If I had gone to school with my old friends, I would probably have gone down the same road they had. Even though Erasmus wasn't the greatest thing going, it taught me how much I needed to depend on God. Every morning as I left for school I prayed, asking God to bring me back home that night. I knew I could get it any number of ways—on the train, in a hallway at school, or maybe somebody would slash me just because they wanted my jacket. But they never did because God was keeping me safe.

"Though there were other Christians at Erasmus, support groups weren't allowed because the teachers were always talking about the separation of church and state. At least we were allowed to sing some of the traditional hymns at Christmas like 'Silent Night,' but not without changing some of the words. For instance, instead of singing 'Christ the Savior is born,' the chorus was instructed to sing, 'He the Savior is born.' But when it came time to sing the song publicly, I closed my eyes and started singing, and before I knew it I sang out the words just like I always had:

We were all sitting down in the funeral parlor when everything exploded around us. Bullets started flying everywhere, and people scattered as fast as they could. My mother and I dove under the nearest pew while my aunt ran downstairs and hid in the casket showroom.

'Christ the Savior is born' and everybody in the chorus just joined in. The teacher was furious, sitting at the piano cursing us out. Afterward she called me into a corner and just went off, threatening to give me a failing grade for the class. Though I didn't fail, I got the lowest grade I ever received in a music class.

Every morning as I left for school I prayed, asking God to bring me back home that night. I knew I could get it any number of ways—on the train, in a hallway at school, or maybe somebody would slash me just because they wanted my jacket.

"Because of the nature of the arts program, there was a lot of pressure to head toward a career in the music industry. My instructors kept telling me I should go on to Broadway. 'You have a great baritone voice. You can fill a room. You don't even need a mike,' they would say. The compliments were nice, but I wanted something else. I felt God calling me to take another path. After I graduated, I was offered a job in the music department at the church. It wasn't a lot of money but I was happy to take it.

"Working with the music of the Brooklyn Tabernacle has been an incredible experience. I always wanted to sing with the choir and always wanted to travel. My job has taken me to Russia and to Jamaica and to places all around the country. Even more, it's given me an opportunity to minister to all kinds of people. Now, whenever I take the mike in my hands, it's not because I love to be on stage. Instead, I pray that God will hide Kevin because Kevin can't save anyone. Only Jesus Christ can do that.

"I used to think that I didn't have a story to tell. I wasn't running around on the streets, wasn't selling drugs, didn't have a drinking problem. Compared to the ways God has worked in other people's lives, my life seemed so tame. Then I started to realize that I did have a story, not so much about how God rescued me but about how he kept me safe. It's a story about God's power to preserve the life that has been dedicated to him.

"My mother made sure that I was dedicated to the Lord when I was just starting out in life. Then she took me to church and taught me about Jesus. When I think about all the parents who have given their children to God, I just want to encourage them that God is still faithful, still able to watch over them. Even if their kids are having a hard time or are going to terrible schools or are threatened by some other kind of danger, I want to tell them not to give up. God can hear their prayers just like he heard my mother's prayers for me. Because what you dedicate to God, he's not going to let go of."

Kevin is right. God is faithful and he is able to keep everything that we give to him. Whether it is our own lives, our families, our problems, our heartaches, or our limitations, God is able to do far beyond what we could ask or think.

As I've traced the course of my life thus far, I see nothing but God's faithfulness, nothing but his love expressed so freely to the little girl too shy to raise her hand in class, to the young pastor's wife who felt so out of place, to the fearful mother watching helplessly as her daughter seemed to slip away from her.

The truth is my inadequacies and fears have been the very place where I've heard the Lord say "stretch out your hand." Over and over, he has led me into situations that have challenged me and stretched my faith beyond anything I could imagine. But that's where I felt his power the strongest.

If there is one theme to the story of my life it is that God is faithful regardless of the circumstances. And his faithfulness is what makes me excited to face the future, whatever it may hold.

What is the part of your life that is shriveled and holding you back from God's best? What is the burden you carry that needs to be given to the Lord in prayer? What fear or complex is stopping you from obeying what you know in your heart is God's will for your life? I hope my story, along with all the others in this book, will challenge you not to give up but to look up in faith to the Lord Jesus Christ. After pouring out his life for you on the cross, will he not also help you to live victoriously as you await the day of his return? God wants to work on your behalf as you turn everything over to him—your life, your wayward child, that mountain of a problem facing you today, the doubt or depression that has plagued you. Let's give everything we have and everything we are to him so we can experience in even deeper ways just how faithful our God is.

The Life God Blesses

The Secret of Enjoying God's Favor

Jim Cymbala
with Stephen Sorenson

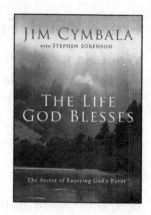

God Wants to Bless Your Life!

Think of what it means to have God bless your family, your relationships, your ministry, your finances ... every aspect of your life. Think how wonderful it would be to have the Creator of the universe "show himself strong" on your behalf.

Good news! That's exactly what he wants to do. God is so eager to bless people that he's constantly searching for that special kind of heart on which he can pour out his goodness. Yours can be that kind of heart.

Pastor Jim Cymbala shares stories from the Bible and from the lives of men and women he has known to reveal inner qualities that delight your heavenly Father. Cultivate them in your heart, and stand amazed as God answers your most heartfelt prayers and makes the impossible come true in your life.

Hardcover: 978-0-310-24202-4
Audio Download, Unabridged: 978-0-310-26159-9

Pick up a copy today at your favorite bookstore!

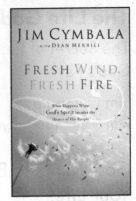

Fresh Faith

What Happens When Real Faith Ignites God's People

Jim Cymbala
with Dean Merrill

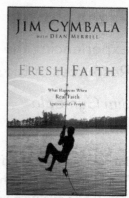

In an era laced with worry about the present and cynicism about the future, in a climate in which we've grown tired of hoping for miracles and wary of trumped-up claims that only disappoint, comes a confident reminder that God has not fallen asleep. He has not forgotten his people nor retreated into semi-retirement. On the contrary, he is ready to respond to real faith wherever he finds it.

Pastor Jim Cymbala insists that authentic, biblical faith is simple, honest, and utterly dependent upon God, a faith capable of transforming your life, your church, and the nation itself.

Jim Cymbala calls us back to the authentic, biblical faith—a fiery, passionate preoccupation with God that will restore our troubled children, our wounded marriages, and our broken and divided churches. Born out of the heart and soul of The Brooklyn Tabernacle, the message of *Fresh Faith* is illustrated by true stories of men and women whose lives have been changed through the power of faith.

Softcover: 978-0-310-25155-2
Audio Download, Unabridged: 978-0-310-26149-0

Pick up a copy today at your favorite bookstore!

Fresh Power

Experiencing the Vast Resources of the Spirit of God

Jim Cymbala
with Dean Merrill

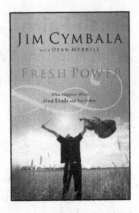

Pastor Jim Cymbala of The Brooklyn Tabernacle has taught his congregation how God's mighty power can infuse their present-day lives and the mission of their church. He continued that teaching nationally in his bestselling books *Fresh Wind, Fresh Fire* and *Fresh Faith*, which tell about the transforming power of God's love to convert prostitutes, addicts, the homeless, and people of all races and stations in life.

Now, in *Fresh Power*, Cymbala continues to spread the word about the power of God's Holy Spirit in the lives of those who seek him. Fresh power, Cymbala says, is available to us as we desire the Holy Spirit's constant infilling and learn what it means to be Spirit filled, both as individuals and as the church. With the book of Acts as the basis for his study, Cymbala shows how the daily lives of first-century Christians were defined by their belief in God's Word, in the constant infilling of his Spirit, and in the clear and direct responses of obedience to Scripture. He shows that that same life in Christ through the power of the Holy Spirit is available today for pastors, leaders, and laypeople who are longing for revival.

Softcover: 978-0-310-25154-5
Audio Download, Unabridged: 978-0-310-26150-6

Pick up a copy today at your favorite bookstore!